J. P. DONLEAVY

J. P. DONLEAVY:

THE STYLE OF HIS SADNESS AND HUMOR

*813
54
DONLEAVY
MAS*

by

Charles G. Masinton

**POPULAR
PRESS**

Bowling Green University Popular Press
Bowling Green, Ohio 43403

Library of Congress Catalog Number 75-930

ISBN: 0-87972-103-0 Paperback

ACKNOWLEDGMENTS

I wish to express my gratitude for permission to quote material from the following works:

The Ginger Man by J. P. Donleavy. Copyright © 1965 by J. P. Donleavy. A Seymour Lawrence Book/Delacorte Press. Reprinted by permission of the publisher.

A Singular Man by J. P. Donleavy. Copyright © 1963 by J. P. Donleavy. A Seymour Lawrence Book/Delacorte Press. Reprinted by permission of the publisher.

The Saddest Summer of Samuel S by J. P. Donleavy. Copyright © 1966 by J. P. Donleavy. A Seymour Lawrence Book/Delacorte Press. Reprinted by permission of the publisher.

The Beastly Beatitudes of Balthazar B by J. P. Donleavy. Copyright © 1968 by J. P. Donleavy. A Seymour Lawrence Book/Delacorte Press. Reprinted by permission of the publisher.

I also want to express my thanks for the financial help provided by the General Research Fund and the Graduate School of the University of Kansas.

Cover design by Lynn Nachbar.

CONTENTS

INTRODUCTION

Since 1955, when he published *The Ginger Man*, J. P. Donleavy has been one of the most widely read contemporary American novelists. His books are reviewed in the major newspapers and magazines of this country, sold (especially in paperback) at bookstores everywhere, and read by people of nearly all professions and backgrounds. In the past few years he has probably been most popular among American college students (along with Joseph Heller, Kurt Vonnegut, and—most recently—Richard Brautigan). But despite great popularity, as well as the high praise he has often received from journalists and reviewers, very little formal criticism has been devoted to his writings. (Most of what has been published deals primarily with *The Ginger Man* and *A Singular Man*, especially the former novel.) The present study is intended to correct that deficiency, in part, by examining in detail both the thematic content and the style of the long works of fiction that have so far appeared—five novels and one novella—and offering an overall assessment of what Donleavy has accomplished in them. Only one of the author's plays and a single piece of short fiction receive critical treatment (because they largely provide the basis for a novel); but the plays, the volume of short fiction, and the essays are included along with the long works of fiction in the bibliography that appears at the end.

Donleavy is like a great many post-World War II American novelists (Heller and Vonnegut might be mentioned again, as well as Thomas Pynchon, Donald Barthelme, and John Hawkes) in his desire to project a private vision of experience rather than depict the manners of a certain social group or render in accurate detail

1

the surfaces of the public world, as the older realists do. He does use various realistic techniques whenever they suit his purposes (he has a precise ear for dialogue and in *The Ginger Man* describes parts of Dublin with great fidelity, for instance); but he approaches fiction primarily as an expressive art and not as a means for faithfully recording his observations of the common, everyday world. Donleavy is doubtless well enough informed about the complex and often frightening social and political realities of our time, but he does not deal with them directly in his fiction. When they appear at all, they are treated obliquely, as they affect or are colored by the sentiments or emotions of one of his protagonists. For it is emotional reality, experience as it is apprehended by the passions and feelings, that arrests Donleavy's attention—and not reality as it is shaped by the intellect. Hence, his fiction concentrates heavily on the subjective lives of his protagonists—on their fears, anxieties, and sorrows on the one hand and on their joys, satisfactions, and longings on the other. (His method for communicating their psychological states to us is the interior monologue, the narrative device that allows them to "tell" their own stories by putting us into direct contact with their stream of consciousness, that welter of sense impressions, memories, feelings, and fantasies comprising their waking mental activity.) Their most painful emotions are the fear of death and the sorrow that comes with the death of a woman they love, and their greatest bliss occurs when they feel wanted and loved by a woman and satisfy their sexual passions. Donleavy's protagonists are all creatures who are guided by their feelings and desires, a fact that is helpful in explaining why Sebastian Dangerfield in *The Ginger Man* (a mischievous, energetic individual ruled by the pleasure principle) is such a vital and interesting character, while the others (who become, with each succeeding book, increasingly morose and withdrawn) tend more and more to be dull and lifeless. This tendency, which is most pronounced in the latest three novels (*The Beastly Beatitudes of Balthazar B, The Onion Eaters,* and *A Fairy Tale of New York*), is a major weakness in them and represents Donleavy's greatest failure as an artist. Conversely, of course, his most notable artistic achievement is the creation of Sebastian Dangerfield, a truly original comic character.

One side of the private vision that Donleavy gives expression to in his fiction is, then, dark and melancholy, clouded over by an obsession with death and a preoccupation with sadness and loneliness. It is this aspect of his worldview that accounts for the growing somberness of his works, an almost palpable mood of dejection that after a time quite obscures the lighter, or comic, element that reflects the other side of his vision of life. Donleavy is best known for his comic talents, and they are his chief asset as a writer. The many pages of comedy in *The Ginger Man*—the bawdy humor, the sly and evasive irony of Dangerfield's speech, the roguish adventures he has—make that novel one of the most entertaining works of fiction in the last quarter-century or so and impart to it a vigor that none of his other works can match. In some fashion or another all the long fictions that follow it are derivative. They use the same narrative strategy, deal with protagonists whose psychological make-up is in certain key respects similar to Dangerfield's, but unfortunately lack the comic intensity and high-spiritedness of *The Ginger Man*. Donleavy's brilliant single inspiration as a writer lives on in that first book, but his repeated attempts to imitate its successful formula have produced works of declining quality and interest. This is not to say that the other novels and the novella are without merit: *A Singular Man* and *The Saddest Summer of Samuel S* sustain a generally high level of literary craftsmanship, and the latter work especially seems to have realized its limited aim (that of dramatizing the sadness, or melancholy, of a middle-aged man who faces life alone and in near-poverty). And the three novels that come after *The Saddest Summer of Samuel S,* especially *The Beastly Beatitudes of Balthazar B,* have passages of crisp humor or great lyrical beauty. But an imitation can never be so good as the original, and the books following *The Ginger Man* do not have the inventive force, the raw energy, or the inspiration that make it a superior piece of fiction.

This last quality—inspiration—may indeed be the clue to Donleavy's foremost problem as a writer. He depends very strongly on inspiration, on the strength of his feelings and emotions, and not on ideas to create fiction. (Thus it is that as the proportion of comedy decreases in his works they become in ever larger measure dependent on mood, on the tone that they can communicate, for their effectiveness.) In *The Ginger Man* joy, anger, frustration, fear, and a wild love of life find their proper expression in the complex, fascinating, lifelike character of Dangerfield. But thereafter Donleavy cannot fuse together the same (or another) dynamic combination of feelings and embody them in a fictional character. The protagonists who are imagined after Sebastian tend to be one-sided because they are characterized almost entirely by their sorrows and disappointments and have less and less of the saving grace of humor (as he does) to make them consistently interesting. In Dangerfield a sense of ironic humor and a fervent will to live complement—and triumph over—the anxieties and the depression he suffers. His multiple qualities make him a well-rounded and arresting figure. But the others have very little of anything resembling his playfulness, unrestrained drive toward self-fulfillment, or quickness of mind and spirit to offset their dolefulness. George Smith in *A Singular Man* is clever as a businessman and witty enough in his litter-writing; Samuel S possesses the wisdom of a failure who has reached middle age; but even these two characters—and certainly those from the next three novels—are presented too much as the victims of melancholy.

If Donleavy's works were informed by intellectual concepts, or were the occasions for him to develop ideas relative to important issues or problems, then they might have displayed greater variety or ingenuity; they might have led him to new sources of creativity after the bright beginning of his first novel. But inspiration could not be extended in full force beyond one book. If *The Ginger Man* can in a sense be called a paean to joy, a celebration of life over death, then the long fictions published subsequently can be seen as odes to dejection or songs of lamentation. (It must be admitted, however, that *A Singular Man* is often funny and that only in its final effect does the humor give way to sadness.) A spirit of vigor or confidence is lost after *The Ginger Man*, and a pervasive gloominess begins to settle over his works. The wonder is that Donleavy has found so many different ways to represent this attitude in fiction. It is equally surprising that his comic sense has persisted in the midst of it and that he has continued to write superb comic dialogue and to invent absurdly funny predicaments for his protagonists.

Lawrence, Kansas   September 1974

I. *The Ginger Man*

Donleavy's most famous novel—and for most critics his best piece of work—is *The Ginger Man*. The author completed it in 1951, but could not find a publisher until 1955, when the Olympia Press in Paris brought it out. An American edition was published in 1958 by McDowell, Obolensky, but this was a revised version omitting the so-called pornographic aspects of the novel. It was not until 1965, with the publication of the Delacorte Press edition, that the full and unexpurgated edition was made available to American readers.[1] Nonetheless, *The Ginger Man* became very popular during the 1950's and is still one of the most widely read post-World War II American novels. A more liberal attitude toward sexual explicitness in the arts has made its scenes depicting the act of love seem rather tame, and very few people today would consider them pornographic. The sections of the novel that once might have seemed offensive are not designed to excite the lust of the reader, but exist to portray more fully the character of the protagonist or to make more credible and concrete the conditions of his existence. The novel will not be remembered so much for the boldness of its subject matter as for its supple, melodious language and its engaging anti-hero, Sebastian Dangerfield.

The Character of the Protagonist

Dangerfield is an American living in Dublin and attending Trinity College on the G.I. Bill a few years after World War II. He meets his wife Marion, a girl from Scotland, while he is still in the

Navy, marries her soon after he is discharged, and begins the study of law. Although Dangerfield plans to inherit his rich father's money after the old man dies, he and Marion live with their daughter Felicity in a state of squalor and poverty. In addition to their economic problems, which are a constant source of friction between Marion and Sebastian, he refuses to study and is sure to fail his law exams. Dangerfield would very much like to pass them and become a successful member of the legal profession, but he spends his time drinking with his disreputable cronies and pursuing attractive women. Marion, a thoroughly conventional girl, detests his laziness and constantly upbraids him for it; but Sebastian, a pagan and wastrel at heart, continues his merry drinking and fornicating. He finds life good when giving expression to the irrational, libidinal side of his nature, which the institutions and rules of culture work to stifle.[2] Dangerfield (whose name denotes the sort of world in which he must struggle to survive) is profoundly obsessed with and afraid of death. And it is his constant awareness of death that prompts him not only to live for the moment and satisfy his appetites but also to run from the many threats he perceives about him in order to live as long as possible. He is a man in flight from death, sees conventional standards of behavior as life-denying, and therefore follows his instincts as the best means of self-fulfillment. His actions, though not always admirable or generous, are a virtual celebration of life in the face of death.

Since he has very little money, Sebastian is forced to live by his wits. He is shrewd, engaging, and always manages—despite some very narrow escapes—to stay a step ahead of those who would force him to conform to society's dictates or submit to their will. In particular, he flees from the responsibilities of husband and father and from the demands of his creditors. (One or two of the funniest episodes come about as Sebastian eludes Egbert Skully, a landlord who chases him all over Dublin to collect unpaid rent on a run-down house that the Dangerfields have vacated.) In his women Sebastian cannot abide too much independence or any habits that might threaten his self-esteem; he prefers the kind of female who will remain loyal despite his occasional brutishness and offer him the solace he needs in times of trouble. Thus he and Marion fail to get along because she violently objects to his unseemly habits and his friends (especially Kenneth O'Keefe, his one-eyed chum from America). And when he is depressed about their poverty or is recuperating from one of his binges, she torments him and criticizes him unmercifully. Early in the novel, for example, she and Felicity return from a visit to her parents to find their home in complete disorder, with wreckage, empty bottles, and stale food scraps everywhere. She sees Sebastian sleeping on the kitchen table and knows that he has been drinking with his "smelly" friend O'Keefe. Marion berates him and finally slaps him when he insults her father, whereupon Sebastian hits her in the face with his fist and tries to smother the screaming Felicity with a pillow. His conduct is not admirable, but he has been driven wild by Marion's shrewish complaining. Marion is portrayed as an unsympathetic character, for the most part, throughout the novel; and when she leaves Sebastian near the end to live permanently with her father and mother, we are not sorry to see her go. We are not wholeheartedly in favor of Sebastian's cruelties and infidelities, by any means, but we come to know his fear and desperation so well that we share his relief in being able to free himself from her.

During the course of the novel Sebastian has affairs with three other women. First, he meets Christine, an English girl working as a laundress in Dublin, and finds that she is both sexually satisfying and pleasant as a companion. The most romantic portions of the book are the few scenes when Chris and Sebastian go about Dublin together and end up making love. But their relationship begins to disintegrate when Sebastian neglects her during an especially desperate period of his life; and though he invites her to go to London with him when he leaves Dublin, she politely refuses. Next, he seduces Lilly Frost, a thirty-four-year-old Irish woman who rents a room from him and Marion. She is extremely shy and proper, and Dangerfield's wiles as he lures her to bed are hilarious. Their affair actually begins when Marion leaves him, and it scandalizes the neighborhood. Lilly, a Catholic who fears telling her priest her sins more than she enjoys committing them with Sebastian, is clearly unsuited as a mate for the Ginger Man.

Dangerfield's most compatible girl friend is Mary, the robust Irish girl he meets at a party in the Catacombs, where his friend Tony Malarkey lives. Mary is Sebastian's sexual equal. She likes him almost immediately, boldly demands that he make love to her, and with no hesitation at all accepts his invitation to go to London with him. Her sexual aggressiveness and insatiability are not seen as immoral but as life-enhancing and healthy. She commits her only fault (from Dangerfield's point of view) when she leaves him and attempts to become an actress in London after Sebastian mistreats her. (When he learns that his father has died and provided in his will that Sebastian receive an annuity of $6000 beginning at the age of forty-seven, he goes berserk and abuses Mary and his friend MacDoon, the leprechaun-like figure who is one of his closest friends in London.) But Sebastian and Mary are reunited on Christmas Eve at a party, and they plan to resume living together and have a baby. Although the novel actually ends with Dangerfield's apocalyptic vision of wild horses running with the soul of a dead person, the principle of life has for the moment triumphed over the forces of death. Sebastian is at least temporarily safe and solvent, having received money from his friend Percy Clocklan, who has mysteriously turned up in London with great wealth after his friends thought him dead. Moreover, Sebastian and Mary will celebrate life when he gives her the baby she craves on Christmas Day. Life energetically, and often desperately, won and sustained in the presence of violence and death: this is the meaning of Dangerfield's vision that suggests itself as he walks toward Mary's apartment in the last scene. The Ginger Man is pursued by death (like the little Gingerbread Boy in the children's tale), but he manages to outwit his pursuer by freeing himself from the grasp of others and acting as an agent of fertility.

Sebastian has an active fantasy life and at times enjoys imagining that he is a fertility figure. His fantasies might generally be understood as attempts to compensate for the poverty in which he lives and the powerlessness he experiences. Thus his most frequent fantasies have to do with great wealth and privilege and a secure position in society, but fertility fantasies are particularly satisfying to him. On one occasion, for example, after Marion accuses him of being distant and cold, he hears her crying in bed at night and comforts himself by imagining that he is a kind of pagan savior in a land filled with distress and suffering:

> Monsters growling from their chains and wailing in the dark pits at night. And me. I think I am their father. Roaming the lane-

ways, giving comfort, telling them to lead better lives, and not to
let the children see the bull serving the cow. I anoint their silver
streams, sing laments from the round towers. I bring seed from
Iowa and reblood their pastures. I am. I know I am Custodian of
the Book of Kells. Ringer of the Great Bell, Lord King of Tara,
"Prince of the West and Heir to the Arran Islands." I tell you,
you silly bunch of bastards, that I'm the father who sweetens the
hay and lays the moist earth and potash to the roots and story
teller of all the mouths. I am out of the Viking ships. I am the
fertilizer of royalty everywhere. And Tinker King who dances
the goat dance. . . . (pp. 70-71)[3]

Echoes of pagan (and especially Celtic) mythology are often
found in Sebastian's fantasies. Their usual function is to support
his vision of himself as a heroic figure. In the scene detailing his
love-making with Chris, he envisions himself as a sort of prelapsar-
ian innocent freeing the laundry girls of Dublin from the influence
of the bishops and leading them, naked, through the streets in a
parade (p. 84). In London, when he goes dringing with MacDoon
and Parnell in a Kangaroo suit and causes a riot in a pub in Soho,
he sees himself and the others as noble Celtic warriors attacking
the stronghold of Cockney louts (pp. 271-272). And during his
last night with Lilly he imagines Jesus as a boon companion of his,
heartily approving of his affair with Lilly (pp. 229-230).

In one or two of his more depressed moments Dangerfield
identifies with Jesus as a suffering or martyred figure or sees himself as a victim of crucifixion. But more frequently he identifies
with St. Sebastian, his namesake, who was shot full of arrows and
beaten with rods for making converts. Another martyr whom he
feels drawn to is Oliver Plunket, an Irish Roman Catholic divine
who was falsely accused of being associated with the "Popish
Plot" of the late 1670's and was hanged, drawn, and quartered.
Sebastian prays to Oliver Plunket in times of distress and publishes
thanksgiving to him in the *Evening Mail* for being delivered safely
away from the scene of a brawl that he has precipitated in a Dublin
pub.

Related to his self-image is Dangerfield's fond wish to live
with dignity. It is his dignity that suffers first when his temper
flares at Marion or when he loses control of himself after drinking
too much. Perhaps his most humiliating experience (and one of

the novel's most memorable comic scenes) occurs in Chapter 10, when Sebastian boards a train for home and forgets to button the fly on his trousers. He does not know that he neglected to put his penis back in his pants when he rushed from the men's room of the train station to board the train, and his embarrassment when he finally realizes why people are staring at him is actue indeed. Many times during the novel he reminds himself that he must keep his dignity; what he fears most (next to death) is the loss of his self-composure. Keeping his dignity is tantamount to preserving his integrity in the face of constant threats from society. We can understand his personality better if we realize that many of his cruel or selfish actions (like hitting Marion or refusing to pay his bills) are responses to attacks on his character or efforts to escape the degrading poverty that his small income guarantees. He strives never to allow himself to experience the sort of personal defeat that his friend O'Keefe suffers. Kenneth, despite his degree in classics, cannot make his way in Europe and finally has to leave Dublin and return to America. Moreover, Kenneth is still a virgin, though he does all he can to find a woman. Dangerfield takes merciless advantage of others and has a successful sex life because his highest goals are self-preservation and personal fulfillment. If he is to maintain a vestige of pride, he must not submit to the self-denying habits of a poor, hard-working student; and if he is to satisfy his personal nature, he must seek the comforts of sex and drink. In short, he rebels against the social code so that he can live a life of joy. He is alienated from society and will be a perpetual outsider because conformity to its rules would rob him of his integrity. The self that Dangerfield struggles to keep intact is an anarchic, Dionysian self;[4] the institutions and customs of his culture would destroy it. His immense discomforts include not only the angst he feels when he thinks of death but also the fear and frustration he has when he experiences societal pressures to conform. He cannot be totally happy in his role as a rebel, for he is denied the security that accompanies conformity and must devise strategems to preserve his freedom. But he does not have to betray his own urges or quash his appetite for life. His instinctive choice to serve the life-giving impulses corresponds to Yossarian's decision in *Catch-22* to escape the horrors of a society in which the individual is robbed of importance by fleeing to Sweden.

Dangerfield's Language and Personal Style

Dangerfield succeeds with women because of his charm, but he works his will on strangers and dupes his enemies by means of his aristocratic bearing and his fake English accent. At the beginning of the novel, when Kenneth visits him, he receives credit for food and liquor from an unsuspecting shop-keeper by appearing before him wearing as a scarf a piece of blue blanket that is the same color as that worn by Trinity College's prestigious rowing team. The feeling of class consciousness that he induces in the man, along with his successful accent, makes it possible for Dangerfield to carry home all he wants from the store. In one episode he goes to the American consulate to pick up his monthly G.I. Bill check and encounters a receptionist who refuses to give it to him without Marion's consent. Sebastian becomes outraged, haughtily calls the girl an "Irish serf," and demands the check. Flabbergasted, she hands it over to him. And on the occasion of his last meeting with Kenneth he has the opportunity to point out to his friend how to express just the right touch of indifference with regard to one's wealth when addressing a member of the working class. Kenneth, who also likes to imagine himself a rich man, makes this announcement to Sebastian:

> "Do you know what my ambition is when I get money? To move into the Shelbourne Hotel. Strut in through the front door and tell the porter would you garage my Daimler for me please."

And Dangerfield answers:

> "No, Kenneth. Would you garage my car."
> "Jesus you're right. That's it. My car. Would you garage my car."
> (p. 218)

Dangerfield is to a degree able to rise above the squalid circumstances of his life and to preserve a sense of his own importance largely through his dignified bearing and speech. Kenneth, of course, is hampered by his inability to use an English accent or adopt a lordly manner and lives a life of noisy desperation.

A part of the reason for Dangerfield's sexual successes is that he assumes a rather gallant and tender attitude toward his women. (When angered, of course, he can be violent and churlish; nevertheless, he prefers to be gentle and quiet in his treatment of them.) He is unassuming and reassuring when he meets Chris, and their going to bed together is made to seem the natural result of a satisfying, happy relationship. As a matter of fact, it is Chris rather than Sebastian who chooses the occasion for making love. When he meets Mary, Sebastian is more adventurous in his courting of her, but they are both guests at Tony Malarkey's party and taking part in a festive activity. Moreover, Mary is the one who asks that they enjoy sex later that night; Sebastian, although he has dared to kiss and woo her, does not act the part of the aggressive lover. With Miss Frost he conducts himself in an extremely decorous manner. By behaving toward her sympathetically and sharing polite conversation with her, he overcomes her shyness and prepares for his conquest of her. He senses that her inhibitions would prevent her from succumbing to a more direct approach, so he slowly gains her confidence by concentrating on the propriety of his talk and actions. (Actually, his proper pose is so exaggerated that it is funny.)

Sebastian deceives Miss Frost and others with his high-born style, but he never deceives himself. He knows that his aristocratic airs are but a mask he wears in order to get along as handsomely as possible in the world. Like the rogue-heroes in other picaresque novels, he must survive by his wit; and he is clever enough to see that in mastering the characteristic gestures of the refined classes and adopting the mannerisms of English speech lie his best defense against poverty, humiliation, and even sexual frustration. (He does not want to destroy society, because he exploits its distinctions and prejudices; he simply wants to be among the privileged or, if that wish proves impossible, to escape the hardships and ignominy of being one of the poor.) That Dangerfield is fully aware of the importance to him of his verbal skills is evident in his comment to MacDoon soon after he arrives in London: "Here I am reduced to accent. No hearth nor home" (p. 263). His wife has left him, he visibly suffers from desperate anxiety, and he is penniless. But he has salvaged some dignity and avoided absolute personal defeat because he still has his way with words.

With Marion Sebastian's speech is unadorned, spontaneous, and often crude; it directly expresses his feelings. Moreover, the idiom he speaks to her is unmistakably American. But with O'Keefe, Clocklan, and MacDoon (and sometimes with his women) a note of jocular formality creeps into his speech. When he is comfortable with friends, the attitude reflected in his talk is typically one of mock-seriousness. In contrast to Kenneth, whose emotional language reveals an inability to distance himself from his troubles, Sebastian's usual playfulness—his employment of understatement, irony, whimsy—gives evidence of an ability to see himself with some degree of detachment. Through verbal artifice—keen-witted speech—he avoids thinking about himself and removes himself sufficiently from his worries to enjoy many moments of his life. His skill with words sets him apart from other men and helps him to maintain the dignified stance that he so urgently requires as a shield against despair. He and his close companions know, of course, that this stance is largely a fabricated matter; but it does grow out of a genuine need of his to be recognized and deemed worthy as an individual.

A typical conversation between Sebastian and O'Keefe will illustrate the value of fine speaking to Dangerfield. During their last meeting together, after Dangerfield has announced his plans to leave Dublin, Kenneth asks him:

> "What about these women of yours when you go to London?"
>
> "Do you think I keep a harem, Kenneth? I lead a life of spartan self-denial. Miss Frost is one of the finest people I know, good Catholic and in every way leads a gainful respectable life."
>
> "Malarkey says the neighbourhood is in disgrace over this affair."
>
> "Miss Frost and I would never stoop. Or set upon one another lasciviously. Within the bounds of good taste and dignity. Furthermore I'd like to point out that Miss Frost is joining the nuns."
>
> "You awful bastard." (pp. 217-218)

Sebastian, it is obvious, is speaking with tongue in cheek. The point to make, however, is that he retains his witty perspective after many difficult days. He is not much better off than Kenneth at this point, but Kenneth has despaired of ever finding love or suitable employment in Europe. Dangerfield, on the other hand, is planning to begin anew in London with Mary. His canniness, energy, and resourcefulness are all reflected in his verbal dexterity and his sense of playfulness when speaking. It is the difference between success and failure for him.

One particularly appealing aspect of Dangerfield's language is the sense of irony it expresses. (This ironic attitude results from his inability to accept conventional values and from the outsider's point of view he adopts toward society.) His ironic detachment is nicely illustrated in the passage quoted above, just as it is in his letter-writing. When he writes to Kenneth in France, his irony takes the form of an elaborate joke or obvious hoax (a transparent "put-on," to use the popular term), which is meant to entertain but not deceive his friend. Dangerfield uses this means to communicate his amusement with life's absurdities and his intellectual superiority to them—an attitude that his crony well understands, though he cannot share it. Kenneth has written Dangerfield about his decision to try homosexuality after being continually rebuffed by women. And Dangerfield gives him this advice:

> About this boy. A most shocking state of affairs. It is not, my dear Kenneth, that I am prude. Far from it. But really, do you think it wise to give up the joys of the heterosexual world without first considering all its possibilities. Grant you, there is no question but that it can be trying and even devastating to endure the celibacy but once you have achieved success, presto, little O'Keefes, just like you. But if you have despaired, if you have the heteroghost, then there is nothing for it but to give yourself with abandon. (pp. 98-99)

Another instance of Sebastian's letter-writing shows him concocting a genuine hoax, with clear intent to deceive. On this occasion his sense of irony is still operative, but it is not meant to be conveyed to the recipients of the letter. Just as he is leaving for England, he receives a letter from his landladies asking about the rent. Dangerfield, prefacing his promise to pay them the rent in the near future, makes these remarks:

It has become incumbent upon me to make an extended business trip to Tangier. I have taken every precaution in closing the house having had a man from Cavandish's to polish and cover all furniture except the hall stand, and a man from a reputable ironmonger's to check the locks on doors and windows.

I know that you must feel a little anxious about the garden and I am sure you will be glad to know I have gotten in touch with the Department of Agriculture to take samples of the soil so that I may have it properly prepared for a spring sowing. As soon as I have their report in my hands I shall have steps taken to have the garden brought up to standard. (p. 240)

The joke resides in the fact that Sebastian is leaving the house in deplorable condition. He has destroyed a desk, pawned some of the contents of the house, and has no intention of ever paying the rent.

Humor in the Novel

Much of the humor of *The Ginger Man* occurs in the very skillful comic dialogue Donleavy writes. Dangerfield's speech is very frequently amusing, but so is that of other characters, especially some of the minor characters. Percy Clocklan, who tells Sebastian about the party in the Catacombs when the two meet in a pawn shop, is especially interesting for the vitality of his Irish vernacular speech. A good example of the humorous dialogue in the book takes place when Sebastian asks him about a most peculiar item he intends to pawn:

"And where did you get that meat?"

"Sebastian, don't breathe a word of this. Now I'm telling you, it's confidential. I had this bird who worked in the butchers. She'd get me as much as eight pounds of the finest steak of an evening. I'd flog three or four pounds and have enough to see me crawling from biddy and lash the rest raw into me gut. See me right for days. I'd give old Tony Malarkey a few pounds now and again for his kids. I was living with him for a while but he's like an oul' hen, clucking around and jealous when I'd come in of an evening laggards. Can't stand to see anyone else enjoying themselves. I bloody well moved out but my woman got caught."
(p. 138)

Clocklan's colorful slang (such as "bird" for girl friend, "flog" for pawn) is as droll as the story he tells. He, like a good many other of Donleavy's characters, is characterized almost completely by his style of speech.

Lilly Frost and Kenneth O'Keefe also come to life for us through their speech. (Donleavy has an accurate ear for the rhythms and intonations of human speech. This talent—along with an ability to populate his novels with a host of interesting comic characters—makes his works quite entertaining. One of the most pleasurable experiences in reading his works comes through our enjoyment of the comic speeches of the principal characters and the lesser figures surrounding them. It should be noted, however, that after *The Ginger Man* Donleavy tends increasingly to give characters other than the protagonist the funny lines to speak.) Miss Frost's reserve, good breeding, and gullibility are indicated in nearly every exchange with Sebastian. In one scene she comes home from work and delicately announces to him that Marion has left him:

"I don't know how to say this, Mr. Dangerfield, but Mrs. Dangerfield told me to tell you that she's not coming back."

"Can you tell me where she has gone?"

"She was very upset and she left without saying exactly, although I understood that she was taking the Liverpool boat and she had a ticket on the train to Edinburgh."

"Rash."

"She was disturbed."

"Couldn't have gotten my gram."

"I don't think she got a telegram."

"No. More's the pity. Avoid this misunderstanding. Rash."

"I'll clean up a little here, Mr. Dangerfield."

"O don't bother, Miss Frost. Leave it to me. I'll take care of it. Desk [the desk he has destroyed with a poker] was a little stuck."

"O no, Mr. Dangerfield, you look so tired. I'll do it. It will only take a minute. I bought some bread and sausages. I think there are a few tomatoes in the cupboard. Would you like to share them with me, Mr. Dangerfield? You must be very hungry."

"I couldn't Miss Frost, it's not fair." (pp. 172-173)

Miss Frost's naiveté and generosity are set in relief against Sebastian's disingenuousness, which he disguises by pretending innocence and surprise. He manages to exploit her sympathetic nature and is soon sharing both her food and her bed.

Donleavy's strategy of portraying character largely through dialogue is probably best seen in this novel in the case of O'Keefe. (Though Dangerfield's character too is realized to a great extent through dialogue, his actions also serve to define him.) O'Keefe's two chief obsessions—sex and money—are constantly reflected in his speech. When he sees Sebastian in the opening scene of the novel, he immediately mentions both of his major problems. The opportunity is given to him by Dangerfield's generous offer of hospitality:

> "Come out. Stay for the weekend. Not much in the way of food but you're welcome to whatever I've got."
>
> "Which is nothing."
>
> "I wouldn't put it that way."
>
> "I would. Since I've arrived here [in Dublin] everything has been down and these guys at Trinity think I'm loaded with dough. They think the G.I. Bill means I crap dollars or a diarrhea of dimes. You get your check?"
>
> "Going to see about it Monday."
>
> "If mine doesn't come, I'll croak. And you're saddled with a wife and child. Wow. But at least you get it steady. And I've never got it at all. Any loose women out there on Howth?"
>
> "I'll keep a watch." (pp. 7-8)

A moment later Dangerfield teasingly adds, "Kenneth, I might have your first woman waiting for you"; and O'Keefe bitterly replies, "Yeah" (p. 8). The hopelessness and frustration that he feels are evident the first time we see him. And the defeat that he eventually accepts is announced in the very tone of his every word.

In addition to the many comic characters that enliven the novel—MacDoon, O'Keefe, Clocklan, Dangerfield himself, and others—Donleavy keeps the momentum of his narrative going through the ample use of comic scenes and episodes. The sense of the world's absurdity that permeates *The Ginger Man* reveals its lighter side in the outrageous conduct of Dangerfield and in the incredible situations he manages to create, just as its more serious aspect shows in the angst he experiences when thinking of death or the seemingly overwhelming demands of society. Among the more satisfying comic incidents are the drunken supper Dangerfield and O'Keefe share on the night before Marion returns from visiting her parents, the embarrassing ride on the train when Dangerfield forgets to button up his fly, and the clever escape he makes from skulking Skully. (In this last incident Sebastian, barricaded in his house against the prowling Skully, slams the front door to make his former landlord think he is trying to escape through it, and then sneaks out the back door unobserved.) It will be noted that these adventures, while humorous, show Sebastian at odds with the conventions and institutions of society—with, respectively, the standards of proper behavior for a husband, the code of decency that governs public conduct, and the part of the social contract that requires the paying of debts. Our amusement is qualified, then, by our realization that for Sebastian life is rarely easy and is often painful. Even the most obviously farcical scenes in the novel—for example, the vivid, hilarious scenes of violence that Sebastian brings about in public houses in both Dublin and London—have a serious side to them. His brawling in the Dublin pub is the end-product of the anger and near-despair he feels when Marion tells him that she has written his father for money and described the wretched circumstances of their lives. Sebastian is convinced that his failure to provide a respectable living for Marion and Felicity will motivate his father to disinherit him. Thus begins a day of drinking that culminates in a fight from which Sebastian must run for his life. The large-scale violence in which he, MacDoon, and Parnell participate in London is part of a happier occasion: they are celebrating the death of Sebastian's father because at this point Sebastian once again expects to inherit a fortune. Aside from the grisly inappropriateness of Sebastian's sentiments, the considerable humor of this incident is somewhat undercut when he later learns that he will not receive a penny for twenty years and in his grief goes berserk for several days.

Black Humor in *The Ginger Man*

When Donleavy mixes comedy, violence, and absurdity in *The Ginger Man*, he frequently produces what has come to be called Black Humor. Black Humor typically occurs when a writer exploits the comic rather than the tragic possibilities latent in the senselessness, the horrors, and the grotesqueness of contemporary life. The humor that results thus often has a cruel or savage, and certainly an ironic, quality about it. The Black Humorist assumes that the world is crazy, that it defies human understanding, that it is, in a word, absurd. Donleavy's humor is by no means solely of this kind, however. There are, for example, many scenes of bawdy humor in *The Ginger Man*; these reflect a fundamentally positive and happy attitude because, despite the crude element in them, they tend to accept life rather than reject or scoff at it. In addition, the sheer fact that Sebastian manages to survive and keep his integrity in a world that both baffles and frightens him stresses the positive dimension of the novel. But a more biting or anxious sort of humor is also present. A good example of it in *The Ginger Man* (one that Bruce Jay Friedman has included in his 1965 anthology called *Black Humor*) is the scene in which the plumbing breaks when Sebastian uses the toilet and the burst pipes spray Marion and Felicity with excrement. The event degrades and disturbs Dangerfield (to say nothing of Marion), but it strikes us as funny because it is so preposterous and surprising. Another example can be found in Sebastian's morbid habit of following funeral processions on his bicycle (which he has purchased for this purpose and painted black) or his practice of watching them from a window of his house. With tongue in cheek he describes his trips on the bicycle in the letter he writes to Kenneth in which he slyly comments on the latter's desire to experiment with homosexuality. And he teases Marion, when she complains about his peering from the window to gaze at passing funerals, by reciting a little verse that mocks the seriousness with which most people observe the death rites. The verse is a parody of the maudlin expressions of bereavement that often are part of a funeral ceremony: "Beyond this vale of tears, there is a life above, unmeasured by the flight of years and all that life is love" (p. 49). His fear of death is a constant burden to him, but he succeeds in developing strategies—

bizarre though they may be—for coping with this fear. These strategies, moreover, are humorous, though they reflect the panic that he feels at the thought of death.

Still other instances of Black Humor are Sebastian's attempt to smother Felicity with a pillow during a quarrel with Marion and his admission to Lilly that he is slowly poisoning a house plant with an eye-dropper. In both cases there is a cruel comic wit present that identifies the humor as "black." Death is often the subject of such grim humor, as can be seen not only in Sebastian's tense maneuverings to allay his fear of dying but also in the pre-occupations of George Smith in *A Singular Man,* who is so stunned by the idea of his own mortality that he constructs a mammoth tomb to house his remains. Many of Donleavy's contemporaries have also chosen to treat the horrors of death from a humorous or cruelly ironic perspective. (For this reason their work is sometimes referred to as "gallows humor.") In John Barth's second novel, *The End of the Road,* a particularly gruesome death of a young woman who is having an abortion is reported with cool detach-ment. In *Catch-22* Joseph Heller makes the wholesale deaths during wartime and the lethal effects of an inhuman bureaucracy seem so absurd as to be without significance—at least until Yossarian realizes with a gasp that the world he lives in is utterly mad. Terry Southern, in *Doctor Strangelove,* represents the paranoia of the Cold War era and global nuclear holocaust as hysterically funny. And Kurt Vonnegut dismisses the awesome fire-bombing of Dresden (where he actually was a prisoner of war at the time) with the aloof, ironic phrase, "And so it goes," in *Slaughterhouse-Five.* Though often motivated by the satirist's impulse to chastise, Donleavy and the other Black Humorists take us beyond the realm of satire, in which human foibles and follies are held up for ridicule and measured against an accepted norm of behavior, into the realm of the absurd, in which the human capac-ity for insane violence and the idiocies of history have outstripped all traditional norms.[5] No established standards of right and wrong are fully adequate to explain life in the mid-20th century. No moralistic injunctions can alert people to the almost incon-ceivable reality of our times. Perhaps only the salutary shock of laughing at contemporary disorders or the surprise of ironic dis-engagement from monstrous actualities that have come to seem commonplace can restore our ethical sense. This, at any rate, appears to be the aim of much Black Humor.

Some Literary Influences and Parallels in *The Ginger Man*

If Donleavy shares some of the concerns and attitudes of the Black Humorists, his work also bears certain resemblances to that of other important 20th-century literary artists. Henry Miller's *Tropic of Cancer* (1934) certainly must be counted as an influence on the writing of *The Ginger Man*. Perhaps the most notable correspondence between the two novels is the bawdiness and the scatological humor they both contain. In addition, they are both told from the point of view of a protagonist who feels complete disdain for the values (and especially the middle-class values) of society and has an insatiable appetite for the pleasures of sex and drink. Both characters are Americans who have left their native land to live in Europe—Miller's protagonist in Paris and Donleavy's in Dublin and London. The lyrical, evocative prose of Sebastian's narrative and the rambling monologue of Miller's persona, with its minute registering of moods and emotions, also have much in common. Another work whose influence can be seen in *The Ginger Man* is Joyce Cary's comic novel, *The Horse's Mouth* (1944). Gully Jimson, the protagonist, is—like Sebastian—a rogue, a lover, a con man who violates every rule but the one that says he must be true to himself. Gully Jimson, in fact, may be the prototype for Sebastian Dangerfield.[6] Moreover, the large cast of comic characters in the earlier work may have suggested to Donleavy the possibility of creating some of the many comic figures in his own book. Donleavy's reading of Franz Kafka also seems to have left its mark on *The Ginger Man*: the projection into fiction of a world that is mysteriously threatening and yet recognizable or even familiar, through which the anxious protagonist must find his way, is a Kafka legacy. (This influence, which is more pronounced in Donleavy's next two long works of fiction, will be discussed at greater length in the chapter on *A Singular Man*.)

Lucky Jim (1953), the comic novel by Kingsley Amis, and John Osborne's play, *Look Back in Anger* (first produced in 1956), cannot be claimed as actual influences on *The Ginger Man*. (Donleavy's novel, it will be recalled, was completed in 1951.) Yet the rather striking similarities in the three works ought to be mentioned. In general, we can observe that the great antagonism toward the social establishment, or certain parts of it, that manifests itself in *The Ginger Man* also characterizes *Lucky Jim* and *Look Back in Anger*. In particular, however, we are struck by the fact that Donleavy's protagonist, who energetically defies convention, strongly resembles Jim Dixon in the novel and Jimmy Porter in the play—both of whom are distinguished by their anti-social conduct.[7] All three young men, in addition, are in their mid-twenties and must compensate for an inferior social standing. (Sebastian differs from the two English characters in having been born a rich American, but in Dublin and London he is quite poor and associates with social outcasts or working-class people.) Jim Dixon, like Sebastian, escapes into fantasy during times of stress; but his fantasies tend to be scenarios in which he acts out his aggressive impulses, while Sebastian's daydreams usually deal with his desire to be rich or heroic. Jim and Sebastian are careless and destructive but also attractively boyish at times. Often they resort to pretense or clever deviousness or to the engineering of a hoax to get what they want. Like Jimmy Porter, they both feel a great contempt for people who consider themselves socially superior. And they both reject academic life, though for different reasons and with different emotions. But it is perhaps the whimsical, irresponsible side of their personalities that makes them seem so similar. In the case of Jimmy Porter and Sebastian, on the other hand, it is the overt violence they are capable of that most clearly reveals their likeness. Both characters are rebellious, unpredictable, full of self-pity, at times quite cruel, and yet very sensitive. They feel put upon and see themselves as the victims of the malice or ill will of others. In their misery and frustration they lash out and are willing to hurt those closest to them. They are particularly brutal to their wives and rail against the families of their wives. Nevertheless, we do not dismiss them with a shrug; we clearly sympathize with Sebastian and even feel an odd kind of attraction to Jimmy because of his vitality and the agony of spirit that causes much of his meanness.

Point of View, Style, and Tone

In *The Ginger Man* Donleavy exhibits a style of writing that becomes his trademark. Despite the anger that surfaces from time to time in the novel, it is written in a lyrical, frequently quite poetic, style that perfectly captures the subtle nuances of mood that Sebastian feels, reveals the complexities and contradictions in his personality, and communicates his deeply sympathetic responses to the natural environment and the changes of season. Much of the writing evokes in us feelings close to those that Sebastian experiences because it is largely the record of his consciousness and powerfully registers his most intimate emotions. The bulk of the novel is rendered as stream of consciousness: most of the actions we see and the impressions we receive are filtered through the mind of Sebastian Dangerfield and presented as his interior monologue. But Donleavy sometimes employs this narrative device in combination with the limited, third-person point of view, for the most part confining himself only to what Sebastian recalls or experiences directly. One of the most salient characteristics of Donleavy's narrative technique is his rapid, unobtrusive shifts from the "I" of the interior monologue to the third-person pronouns of the limited point of view. Because the focus is kept on Dangerfield's perceptions and mental activities, however, we are hardly aware of the pronoun-changes; and this unusual practice gives us the illusion of viewing Dangerfield both from "within" and "without," as it were, at the same time.

Part of the lyrical quality of the prose comes from Donleavy's strong preference for the present participle verb form and the frequency with which he uses sentence fragments. The present participles give the writing a singing, flowing quality; and the sentence fragments—which usually correspond to the hectic but alert workings of Sebastian's mind—keep us attuned to his every sensation and thought. Thus we are immersed in the emotional life of the protagonist and feel the pathos of his struggles and suffering. Donleavy's devotion to the subjective experience of Sebastian—his many moods, the welter of impressions that flicker across his consciousness, his aching passions—imparts a lyric intensity to the writing that is very close to poetry. This affective quality in the prose, along with Donleavy's fondness for colorful diction and phraseology in his characters' dialogue and his habit of ending a chapter with little verse tags, reveals an extraordinary poetic sensibility. A useful passage in which to demonstrate Donleavy's poetic style is the opening paragraph of Chapter 3, a typical example of Dangerfield's interior monologue. Dangerfield is sitting on the sea-cliff in back of his house the morning after he and Kenneth have had dinner together. We are aware of not only the impressions on his mind that the romantic scene makes but also the pensive mood that it instills in him:

> The sun of Sunday morning up out of the sleepless sea from black Liverpool. Sitting on the rocks over the water with a jug of coffee. Down there along the harbor pier, trippers in bright colors. Sails moving out to sea. Young couples climbing the Balscaddoon Road to the top of Kilrock to search out grass and lie between the furze. A cold green sea breaking whitely along the granite coast. A day on which all things are born, like uncovered stars. (p. 18)

The present participles give a melodious touch to this peaceful, meditative passage and also introduce a sense of movement into it. In addition, its concreteness makes it very vivid and memorable.

As the above excerpt shows, the tone of Donleavy's prose can be tender and wistful. It can also be quite melancholy, as it is when Sebastian reflects on the passage of time or thinks of death. Once, for example, when he and Marion are making love, he is struck by a sense of irreparable loss. During the act of love he is reminded of a girl friend he had in America long ago and recalls that she died in an auto accident:

> We were rich. So rich we could never die. Ginny laughed and laughed, white saliva on her teeth lighting up the deep red of her mouth, fed the finest food in the world. Ginny was afraid of nothing. She was young and old. Her brown arms and legs swinging in wild optimism, beautiful in all their parts. She danced on the long hood of her crimson Cadillac, and watching her, I thought that God must be female. . . . Ginny had driven her long Cadillac through the guard rails of a St. Louis bridge and her car shone like a clot of blood in the mud and murk of the Mississippi. (p. 51)

The first part of the passage is joyous, but an elegiac quality trans-
fuses the joy because Sebastian's memories are fixed on the fact of
the girl's death.

The note of sadness or melancholy is balanced against the
ribaldry and comedy in the work to give Dangerfield's life a
seriousness and a poignancy that it otherwise would not have. He
is, of course, first and foremost a comic character. And the
picaresque form of the novel—with its episodic structure dominated
by a rogue-hero rushing from one breathless adventure to the next
—certainly maximizes his comic potential. But Donleavy is not
content to let us view his protagonist from a distance and laugh at
his lunatic ways as if he were no more than a clownish figure.
Part of the design of the novel involves our being made to sympathize with and recognize the humanity of a rascal whose actions
constitute an assault on some of our most cherished moral and
ethical precepts. Dangerfield is knavish and unprincipled, but he
also displays such vitality, humor, and love of life that he finally
wins our favor. And since he suffers greatly too, we are even less
inclined to judge him harshly. It is chiefly through the point of
view, however, that we achieve a sympathetic understanding of
him as a character: by using the interior monologue, Donleavy
draws us directly into his mind and makes us experience the world
very much as he does. Donleavy is so successful in his lyrical
evocation of Sebastian's moods and feelings that they become,
in effect, our own. Thus the tone of the writing is an important
index to our understanding of Sebastian because it creates an emotional bond between him and us.

As we feel both his ecstasy and gloom, the sting of his disap-
pointments, and the elation of his freedom, we come to know
Donleavy's most interesting and most fully realized character.
Sebastian holds a prominent place among the outstanding fictional
figures of Donleavy's literary generation: Saul Bellow's Herzog,
Ralph Ellison's Invisible Man, Joseph Heller's Yossarian, and John
Updike's Rabbit. Like the Ginger Man, they all face the unnerving
problems of the world as envisioned in the years shortly after
World War II. It is a world that threatens to close in on them, to
suffocate them with its demands and its confusion, to rob them
of their sanity or identity. Their problem is to learn to live in it
without losing either their humanity or their individuality.

II. *A Singular Man*

Donleavy's second novel, *A Singular Man* (1963), is in several respects like *The Ginger Man*. Both are comic works with strong elegiac overtones, both deal with a protagonist who is preoccupied with death and in flight from the indignities visited upon him by the world, and both make use of a stream-of-consciousness narrative style. (As is the case in *The Ginger Man,* Donleavy's handling of point of view is deliberately inconsistent. He typically jumps back and forth from the "I" of the interior monologue of George Smith, through whose eyes we receive most of the impressions of the novel, to the limited, third-person point of view. Again, the first-person pronouns allow us to perceive the world through the central character's consciousness, while the rapid shifts to the third-person pronouns permit an almost simultaneous "outside" view of him.) In addition, the protagonist of each novel finds solace and freedom from worry in sex. Both characters also share the need to keep up the appearance of propriety—no matter what ridiculous situation they may have precipitated—so as to avoid the agony of humiliation and embarrassment.

But there is one major difference in the personalities of George and Sebastian. While they are both loners who feel out of place in a world filled with uncertainty, Smith does not respond to his situation with the aggressiveness or the zany daring of Dangerfield. Sebastian can always bluff his way out of a difficult situation, but the protagonist of *A Singular Man* tends toward passiveness and to a greater degree accepts his role as a victim of life's vicissitudes. Still, he is far from helpless. He is a successful businessman and a millionaire (a fact that radically sets him off from Dangerfield). In his private life, however, he must be counted a failure. He and his wife have separated, he receives no joy from his children, and his affairs with his secretaries, Miss Martin and Sally Tomson, ultimately leave him with a greater sense of loss and loneliness than he has ever known. He finds real love and affection in his relationship with Sally, but he is married and has no hope of a permanent arrangement with her. Moreover, she dies in an auto accident at the end, leaving him desolate and crushed.

The Representative Quality of the Novel

A Singular Man records George Smith's fumbling attempts to find rest from his anxieties and an escape from the malice of his fellow-men. From Sally he receives the sort of love and comfort he needs as a defense against the world, but their relationship is doomed from the beginning. As he does in *The Ginger Man,* Donleavy here offers us a story of a man's frustration in his attempts to realize his fondest dream. George wants love and acceptance; despite his great wealth, however, he very rarely has his wish. And Sebastian, who has no trouble finding female company, needs and longs for his father's fortune to rescue him from a life of poverty. But his wish too is crushed. In these two novels Donleavy dramatizes the impossibility of permanently possessing both love and money, and in *A Singular Man* he takes the old theme of the rich man's inevitable disappointment in love and expands it into a sort of parable of the plight of a typical man in the present age.

The story of Smith (whose name is so common as to make him a modern Everyman) is meant to have universal application.[1] It is not until the last few pages, when Grand Central Station is mentioned, that we know with certainty that the location of most of the action is New York City. The urban environment that we glimpse through George's consciousness at times suggests New York, but no actual streets or buildings are named until Grand Central Station is identified. Our strongest impressions are those of a menacing large city in which the protagonist must avoid a multitude of dangers in order to conduct his business and get on with his life. The names of places and people that Donleavy chooses create a feeling of indefiniteness about the location and help us to realize that the events in the novel could be occurring anywhere. George lives in Merry Mansions, goes to work in his little office at 33 Golf Street, and belongs to The Game Club, where he works out and takes fencing lessons. After a time he moves his office to Dynamo House on Owl Street, but even there he cannot avoid the threatening letters that come from J.J.J. and The Associates. We never learn exactly what business George oversees; we know only that he has made a fortune at what he does and that he is an independent operator. Even his secretaries do not know much about his work. Their main job seems to be answering the disturbing letters and filing them away. (George's answers are a high point of the comic art in the novel. Though he is shy and fearful, he always manages to be flip and insulting to J.J.J.) Both his offices are small and bare; they reveal no hint of his commercial activities. Like the generalized place-names, the mysterious operations George manages produce a sense of indefiniteness in the reader, an uncertainty that removes the story from the realm of the particular and suggests that its implications are general. We are to understand that George's harried life as a businessman makes him universally recognizable and therefore typical. The taxing strain that he feels as a put-upon executive seeking to stay ahead of the competition in business makes him a representative man of the modern era. His world is our world, and his reactions to it are those that we either have shared or witnessed. Whichever is the case, we can sympathize with him. His intense suspicion (it often amounts to paranoia),[2] his desire for a place of rest and peace, and his obsession with death all identify him as a man of our time. Thus what befalls him in some measure throws light on our predicament.

In other ways too the story of George Smith is meant to be typical. He has become hard and cold, as his friend and alter ego Bonniface reminds him, in order to make money. Success in business has not brought him happiness or friends. He was once poor and well liked, we learn, but chose to stifle his warm-hearted nature so that he might rise in the world. Some years before the opening of the novel he journeyed from the Old World (the place seems to be Ireland, but we cannot be sure) to find his fortune in the New World, leaving his poor, gentle parents behind him. (His life exemplifies the poor-boy-makes-good theme that is so much a part of the American Dream.) Since that time George has, apparently, been too preoccupied with his own efforts to be a success to stay in touch with his mother and father, because he is shocked and saddened when he learns of their death early in the novel. In addition, his marriage has disintegrated, and his three children treat him disrespectfully when he visits them during the Christmas season. (It must be pointed out, however, that the disastrous flaws in the marriage are not really his fault. His wife Shirl is a grasping, hysterical, and thoughtless person who is too egotistical to love.) In short, he is alone and very, very sad.

To compensate for his loneliness, his fears, and the abuse he suffers, he has started to build an enormously large and expensive mausoleum for himself in Renown Memorial Cemetery. (He uses the name of Doctor Fear so that people will not trace the building to him—but to no avail.) It is the largest such structure ever planned by the director of the Cemetery, and it outrages almost everyone who knows about it. Shirl would like the money going into its construction, the population in general considers him odd and probably mad for undertaking the project, and the press keeps the place under surveillance in order to take pictures of him when he visits his mausoleum. So even this scheme, which he hopes will bring him a little of the dignity and respect that he sorely craves, fails him. Instead, it alienates him more than ever from his wife and makes him a topic of public gossip. But he persists in his plans for the huge tomb, and near the end of the novel he sends out invitations to a reception celebrating its completion. Ironically, the reception does not materialize. Bad weather causes its postponement, Sally dies in a car wreck, and Smith attends her funeral instead. His life is now barren, and the work closes on a note of deep melancholy. As we reflect back on the novel, we realize that a somber, elegiac tone has suffused even the humorous passages. There are many hilarious comic scenes and characters in A Singular Man, but Donleavy has created comedy in the face of sorrow, loss, and the ever-present reality of death. The gigantic tomb and Sally's death remind us of what George never forgets.

Comic Aspects of the Novel

Some of the most notable comic scenes dramatize George's sad but funny sex life. After he is insulted by Shirl on his trip to bring Christmas presents to her and his children, he returns to the little rural hotel (The Goose Goes Inn) near her house to be alone and salve his wounds. But she follows him there and entreats him to make love to her. Making love is difficult for him because of the long underwear he has on. (Its red color has earlier called forth Shirl's derisive comments.) But the garment bothers him less than Shirl's request that he hurry because she has friends waiting downstairs to take her to a party. Enraged, he throws her out of his room, only to endure his solitariness again.

On another occasion George takes Miss Martin to his cabin in the woods to escape the newspaper photographers who have been following him. Located on the Worrisome River, a few miles from Cinder Village, it is (or so he hopes) the perfect retreat. When she finds that she will be alone with him for a day or two, Miss Martin balks at the idea of staying in the cabin. But she soon relents, largely because she does not want to ride back home all alone with the chauffeur and explain to her mother that she has lied about attending a chaperoned weekend party. When it is time to go to bed, Smith takes the couch in the drawing room and leaves his bedroom for Miss Martin. But (as he has foreseen) she is frightened by one of the large spiders that inhabit the cabin and runs to him for protection during the night. They are both naked, and the expected love-making takes place. Despite the blissful night spent together, George refuses to let her call him by his first name the next day. A tender exchange of caresses is fine, but the proper relationship between boss and worker must be maintained. Naturally she is hurt and angered (as we would expect her to be); George, however, insists that she has no reason for addressing him familiarly.

A few months later he learns that Miss Martin is pregnant. When he does not respond to her announcement that she is going to have his child, she picks up the rifle with a hair trigger that she has brought with her to work and threatens to shoot him. He finally has to tackle her to disarm her, and in the meantime he has been reduced to begging for his life. Moreover, she has caught him wearing no trousers and suffering from a hangover. (He has been napping on the couch in his office, trying to sleep off the effects of the wild night before, when he drank too much and slept with Queen Evangiline, his friend from the Old World who taught him about sex during his young manhood. She is old enough to be his mother—as Sally sarcastically points out when he brings the Queen to Sally's engagement party—but she is still quite attractive.) The idyll in the woods, so innocent from George's point of view, has a typical result for him—confrontation with death.

The idea that even love is no escape from death is best illustrated, of course, in his affair with Sally. When he leaves the cabin with Miss Martin to attend a party at the estate of Mr. Jiffy (whose initials are J.J.J., the same as those on the ominous letters), he meets Sally, who has not been to work for weeks. Smith has fallen in love with her and has missed her terribly, and meeting her at the party thrills him. She brings her enormous dog Goliath with her, and Jiffy shoots the animal when Goliath fights with his own dogs and threatens to disrupt the gathering. In her shock and dismay she asks Smith to take her away, and he leaves Miss Martin to look after herself. Though the occasion is a sad one, the drive to the hotel where they spend the night together is quite funny. First, Smith, who is driving Sally's fancy sports car on the wrong side of the road, causes an accident with another motorist. He flees from the scene of the accident and gets lost. Then he awakens a farmer because he needs a telephone to make reservations at the hotel and nearly gets shot by the farmer. His ineptitude has precipitated one hilarious episode after another.

The night spent at Hotel Boar (occurring at mid-point in the novel) is George's happiest time. He is with the person he cares for the most and has no greater ambition than to pass the rest of his days with her. But the romantic scene is also quite humorous. In amazed delight Sally exclaims at the large size of Smith's penis, and when they have consummated their love, Smith tells her the side-splitting story of his adventure with Bonniface during their stay at the university. Bonniface is caught cheating on an examination, but he is not disgraced because of extenuating circumstances leading up to his unethical action. He and George decide to celebrate his good fortune; they get drunk, wander into a storeroom full of ale, and consume bottle after bottle of it. When Bonniface needs to relieve himself, he urinates out the window. The breeze carries his urine into a window downstairs, and he douses an old couple who are asleep. More ribaldry follows as the old woman, who is incredibly coarse, charges up the stairs after them and attempts to thrash Bonniface. Donleavy's comic gift is very evident in farcical scenes like this because they give him the opportunity to write the clever and sometimes risqué dialogue for which he is justly praised and to create a wide variety of humorous characters. (Since his novels are loosely organized, it is possible for him to include extra comic scenes of this sort without damaging the overall plan of the works. If he followed the conventions of the well-made, realistic novel, which call for plausibility and a logical progression of events, the comic sequences and characters that add so much of the zest to his writings would be considered extraneous unless they contributed directly to the development and resolution of the plot. As it is, their success as individual units within the larger framework of the novels provides the only justification he needs for including them.)

The comic dialogue in *A Singular Man* (like that in *The Ginger Man*) is a constant source of entertainment and a demonstration of Donleavy's immense talent for mimicking actual speech patterns. Moreover, it is a very important means by which the author dramatizes character in both novels. The rapid exchange between Smith and Miss Martin, when the latter announces her pregnancy, works especially well to reveal character and produce laughter. She turns the rifle on Smith, and he responds:

> "Miss Martin what are you doing with that gun."
>
> "Listen to me."
>
> "I'm listening. Put the gun down."
>
> "No."
>
> "Miss Martin. I hope you're aware of what you're doing."
>
> "I am, you're not going to turn rat on me."
>
> "I beg your pardon."
>
> "No you're not."
>
> "Miss Martin get a grip. For God's sake."
>
> "My finger's on this trigger, that's all I need."

"Do you realize you could shoot me."

"Yes."

"All right. Put it down then."

"You think it's a joke."

"I don't think anything's a joke. Just want to find my paper bag." [He has been searching for a paper bag full of money, not recalling that he threw the contents down from the rooftop of the Queen's hotel the night previously.]

"You didn't even hear what I said. I said I was pregnant. Over three months."

"This is no time to be hysterical. My eyeballs are rusted in the sockets. I feel terrible, what a hangover. And I can't find my paper bag." (pp. 221-222)[3]

Another example of successful comic speech (in a scene not nearly so frustrating to Smith) is the brief conversation George has with the clerk working at the hotel where the Queen is staying. George, drunk, has been searching everywhere for her, and the clerk is suspicious of this odd person who has just entered the lobby:

"Perhaps sir, you've got a reservation."

"Perhaps I haven't."

"What have you got."

"I beg your pardon. Are you being forward."

"Sir, I'm trying to be of assistance."

"Her Royal Huzzy the Queen."

"I beg your pardon, sir."

"I wish to be connected."

"Have you a prior connection."

"I beg your pardon."

"Sir, I mean are you expected." (p. 216)

The dialogue is humorous principally because the air of propriety the two men try to maintain not only prepares for their unintended use of double-entendre, but contrasts so markedly with it and the farcical "Her Royal Huzzy" as well.

An aspect of Donleavy's comic talent that relates closely to his inventive and amusing dialogue is his ability to burlesque certain styles of writing or speaking. In the course of *A Singular Man* he offers absurd parodies of the letter-writing style of lawyers and businessmen and the style of newspaper reporting. His achievement lies in the skill with which he exaggerates the use of deadening clichés, stilted language, and grammatical errors for humorous effect. First, here is an excerpt from a letter from Sun Shine & Son, the legal counsel of one Harry Halitoid of Fartbrook, who is suing Smith for knocking him onto the subway tracks and injuring him. (Actually, it is Halitoid who starts the fight with Smith as they are waiting for the subway train, but everyone soon believes that Smith assaulted the man, including the newspaper reporter who covers the incident.) The awkwardness and the wildly improbable neologisms ("knockment," "spoilment") as well as the circumstances described convey a sense of the ridiculous:

Dear Sir,

On a Wednesday of the 19th ultimo, at 3:34 P.M. (approx.) o'clock at Battery Station of the Rapid Transit system of this city you made an unprovoked and savage attack upon our client, Mr. Harry Halitoid which resulted in a knockment into the tracks of the said system where there was a sustainment of considerable head and body injury.

Therefore and in view of the heretofore we furthermore establish that our client who is positioned as a master Boiler Watcher at a prominent hospital where many wealthy people have been treated has been unable to preside at work for two weeks, during which the hospital steam has been making unfamiliar pounding noises in the pipes upsetting the inmates and our client himself has been under the care of doctors and night nurses, one of whom is a specialist in soft foods. The upper incisors as well as one canine and one bicuspid are missing from our client's jaw, obliging him to eat slops. . . .

By way of damages we are asking a sum to offset the physical and mental distress endured by our client as well as making good the suit of clothes which suffered spoilment in the tracks. . . . (pp. 192-193)

Legal language is also—but more ambitiously—parodied in Smith's will (which he calls his "last will and testicle") on pp. 99-101.

However, it might be well to remember that Smith himself is the author of this tongue-in-cheek document. Note, for example, his archness in this sentence:

> All my chattel possessions whatsoever remaining gripped in my lunch hooks at the time of stepping into darkness, which I do not care to have herein mentioned as the eternal shid, there having been a sufficiency of same throughout my casual meander through life, are to be held to public auction. (p. 100)

Like Sebastian, he is a past master at using sly affectedness and irony in his writing.

The way Donleavy ridicules business communications is nicely illustrated in the brief letter Smith receives from J.J.J. on p. 102. Its ribald opening is a characteristic of the letters found in Donleavy's works:

1 Electricity Street

Rear Room
604

Dear Sir,

    To hand your letter of "Turdsday" so unseemly spelled, in which you threaten us with the words "Watch out" and the postscript that you are blessed with two headlamps to focus on our medical history.

    We now require by telegram that you send us something to salve the outrage caused by these recent remarks to this office.

Yours faithfully,

J.J.J. Jr.

This letter, like virtually all the others sent or received by Smith as he conducts his business, is a masterpiece of irrelevance. The main purpose of these missives seems to be the communication of threats and insults to the competition. They offer lively entertainment, of course, and constitute a satiric commentary on the letter-writing style often associated with the business community.

The aspects of newspaper reporting style that Donleavy parodies are its concern with trivia and its perfectly serious approach to the most unlikely or grotesque events. In the account of George's confrontation with the obnoxious man in the subway, moreover, Donleavy probably intends to ridicule a practice that news reporters are sometimes accused of—the misrepresentation of facts. As can be seen from the two paragraphs quoted below, George is held to be the aggressor in the incident:

ENGINEER SUES TOMB BUILDING FINANCIER

OVER SOCK IN SUBWAY.

A summons was issued today against Mr. George Smith formerly of 33 Golf Street and removed to Dynamo House, Owl Street where he was traced. The victim Mr. H. Halitoid of Fartbrook claims he was the innocent recipient of a right hook to the jaw in the rapid transit while his attention was distracted with other passengers watching a rat gambol down the tracks. As he and other spectators on the Battery platform (uptown side) waited for the rodent to be electrocuted, Mr. Halitoid alleged a fist encased in a knuckle duster thundered out of space and (according to his doctors) landed on his lower mandible scattering bicuspids everywhere.

Interviewed at his bedside this morning, Mr. Halitoid declared that terror was rampant in this city and asked this reporter, "Are our rights to be protected or must we walk in fear outside our homes." (p. 201)

The incongruity of the business about the rat in a story that purports to be serious is naturally humorous, but humor also results from the unfortunate mixture of levels of usage. The usual plodding formulas of newspaper writing combined with slang ("knuckle duster," "right hook to the jaw") and an unsuccessful, pretentious attempt at elevated diction ("mandible," "bicuspids," "gambol") is jarring. Donleavy's handling of these elements, of course, makes a fine burlesque of newspaper reporting.

Black Humor in *A Singular Man*

The Black Humor in *A Singular Man* grows out of the same vision that informs Donleavy's other works—the vision of an absurd world. In an absurd world the individual is profoundly alienated from his surroundings, his fellow creatures, and often himself. He wants his life to have meaning and order, but it presents him with a picture of chaos.[4] He is a stranger wherever he goes, and even if he can make progress in certain of his endeavors, death stands ready to undo all he has achieved. (This is the case for both George Smith and Sebastian Dangerfield, though Sebastian's anxiety at the thought of death is perhaps greater than George's. The world George lives in is nightmarish, unsafe; people are unfriendly and unpredictable; threats to his safety and happiness are everywhere; and nothing he does insures the peace or love he desires.) One possible reaction to this worldview is sorrow and regret, which we find manifested in the elegiac strain that infuses Donleavy's works and tends to dominate the later fictions. Another possible reaction is the sort of bitter (i.e., "black") humor that is partly ironic amusement at the grotesque horrors of everyday life and partly anger and disappointment that the world does not conform to man's ideals. This too we find in Donleavy, and it helps to explain the furious rebellion of Dangerfield and the fact that he and the protagonists in the other long fictions feel little loyalty to social custom and community standards of behavior. They are thrown on their own unaided resources not only to withstand the shocks of existence but also to find whatever satisfactions they seek. Thus it is not surprising that Sebastian finds relief from his miseries in following his instincts. They also ultimately prove unsatisfactory, but at least the instincts guard against the forces of repression instituted in society. George, whose life is no less conditioned by a sense of danger and displacement than Sebastian's, leads a more conventional existence only in the sense that he occupies a successful position in society as a businessman. In all other ways he is "singular": he is eccentric, antisocial in his habits, deeply suspicious of people (usually with good reason), and full of anxiety. He is convinced that the only way to get along is to erect a barrier between himself and others. Thus he affects a rigid, formal manner of speaking; refuses to speak to an old school chum and in general avoids people; and buys a bullet-proof car—as much to insulate himself from insult and unfriendliness as to guard himself against gunfire. But his attempts to maintain a dignified exterior make him ridiculous and generate much of the humor of the novel.

The mausoleum he is building for himself must also be seen

as an attempt to shore up his dignity. Death is a very real thing in his world, and he tries to confront it seriously, as befits a man in his position. Yet the tomb that is meant to bring him an increased sense of self-importance is also a reminder of death, and Smith cannot escape from the knowledge of his own helplessness and insignificance. Moreover, the tomb is an exceedingly large building, a pretentious edifice that is more a monument to his fear than it could ever be a memorial to his accomplishments. The great gulf between Smith's illusion that his final resting-place will insure his dignity and the actuality of its grotesqueness is the area of the absurd. And of course this large area is fertile ground for Black Humor. In the last analysis Smith's obsession with death is funny, even though death itself is the most horrifying of realities. The element of fear found in much Black Humor is certainly here. That which terrifies (death) and that which amuses (George's ostentatious mausoleum) are expressions of a single, ironic sensibility in the Black Humorist. This sensibility includes an awareness of the frightening absurdities of contemporary life and an impulse to laugh at them as well. Something is won for the human spirit when laughter rather than resignation or panic is possible.

Many events and circumstances other than death receive the Black Humorist's touch in Donleavy's works, but death is dealt with at some length here because Donleavy recognizes it as the ultimate absurdity, that which erodes the significance of all human accomplishments and plans. Some of the other absurdities that George has to contend with are his unregenerate eccentricities (his "singularities"); his isolation from normal human relationships, and in particular the separation from his family; and his inability to come to terms with the madness and malice he perceives about him. (His eccentric personality and his isolation explain why so much of the space of the novel is devoted to his reflections and memories—his "inner" life. It should be noted, in this regard, that George is not only alienated from other human beings, but also experiences a psychological reality that is at wide variance from the self that he tries to project in his activities as a businessman. Or, to put the matter another way, there is a deep division between the shy, insecure George that we know from his internal monologues and the proper, self-assured appearance that he tries to maintain in the presence of others.) George is not at ease in the world—he does not feel at home in it; and his strategies for keeping his psychic balance (retaining his composure, coping with the confusion in his life) make him an ironic and laughable figure.

Donleavy's Use of the Double

The function of Bonniface in the novel must be defined before we can fully understand the character of George. Bonniface is his alter ego, his Double, and represents the "shadow" side of his personality. In *The Ginger Man, A Singular Man,* and *The Beastly Beatitudes of Balthazar B* Donleavy provides the protagonist with a close friend who, although different from him in important ways, is nevertheless also very much like him in key respects. So close are they, in fact, that this intimate friend (or bosom buddy, as he would be called in popular parlance) and the protagonist himself seem to be the two halves of a single personality. If the Double embodies certain characteristics that are the opposite of those that distinguish the protagonist, the two are nevertheless joined together by mysterious but unbreakable bonds. In all three novels, moreover, they attend school together and share many of the same aims, desires, and fundamental values. But the Double-figure fails in some crucial way that sets him off from his companion. Thus, unlike Sebastian, Kenneth fails to satisfy his sexual urges and lacks his friend's brazen wit to make his way in Dublin and on the Continent. Bonniface is saintly (as his name suggests) but poor; George, on the other hand, is stingy and rich. Beefy (Balthazar's Double in *The Beastly Beatitudes of Balthazar B*), who is bold, randy, and irreverent, loses his inheritance; Balthazar, who is shy and withdrawn, keeps his fortune. The Double functions as an artistic projection of the unrealized or repressed side of the protagonist's personality. He therefore not only represents the personal qualities of the protagonist that have been denied expression, but also serves as a reminder of the kind of person the latter might have become.[5]

Bonniface and George go to college together, marry and have children at about the same time, and go out into the world together expecting happiness and fulfillment. But then their lives begin to follow different courses. George, the son of poor people, makes a fortune, while Bonniface loses his wealth and social position. Still, Bonniface's nobility of spirit never leaves him, as George well knows; but George, afraid of what might happen to him if he is tender and kind, adopts a cold and calculating manner. The poverty and degradation that Bonniface experiences convince him that he cannot be so generous and open as his friend. That George fears sharing Bonniface's lot is indicated in George's desire to avoid Bonniface when the latter comes to America seeking financial help from his old college chum. George admires Bonniface and is drawn to him, but at the same time he is distressed by something about his friend and wants to run from him. He instinctively recognizes something of himself in Bonniface, and the good man's misery both fascinates and repels him. When George and Miss Martin are staying at the cabin in the woods, George thinks he sees Bonniface peering in through a window and is thrown into panic. But in actuality Bonniface is not there; the image seen through the window (p. 133) is only George's hallucination. George later realizes that what he saw was a "mirage at the log cabin window" (p. 255); at the cabin, however, he is distraught and leaves immediately with Miss Martin to go to Jiffy's party.

There are other indications too that Bonniface must be seen as George's Double. The story George tells Sally about Bonniface's urinating out a window is duplicated when George visits the Queen the night he throws the money off her roof. On this occasion he also urinates off the roof—to the Queen's annoyance. And just as George knocks Harry off the subway platform onto the tracks, Bonniface hits a man who is bullying him onto the subway tracks. Their closeness is further revealed in the fact that Bonniface seems to know everything about his friend, both in the past and in the present. Bonniface is truly George's second self, but the millionaire chooses to insulate himself from the conditions that Bonniface endures because he cannot bear to accept the possibility of poverty and indignity in an uncaring world. Bonniface accepts with grace his stinking apartment, his low-paying job at the airport, and his diminished prospects; and still he has the goodness to pick up a stray dog, whom he names Mr. Mystery, and care for him. George, on the other hand, is aghast at even the thought of having less than regal dignity and respect.

After Bonniface comes to America, George first sees him at the Jiffy estate. He searches everywhere for Bonniface and finally finds him with a maid in an ice house far beneath the kitchen. The long descent into the cold, musty room suggests a journey into the realm of the unconscious, the "underside" of the personality, which is the appropriate place for George to locate his "shadow." George's last view of Bonniface occurs at the airport and clearly reveals the fascinated horror with which George regards him. George has not helped him out of his poverty, and Bonniface has become more and more desperate. He is on the verge of total collapse and seems ready to despair. In his coldness of heart it is almost as if George were "killing" the self represented by Bonniface. He watches Bonniface at work at the ticket counter, unable to perform his duties competently, every few minutes leaving to go to the men's room. Eventually George decides to follow him to bid him good-by. Bonniface is not in any of the stalls, and it takes an uncomfortably long time for George to find him. He finally has to look in a mop closet, and he sees Bonniface pouring red wine into his mouth from a bottle, letting it flow all over his head and face and Smith's sable coat, which he has asked to wear. Smith leaves him in the closet, a wretched, broken, forsaken human being. Wearing Smith's coat, he seems more than ever to be the part of Smith that the protagonist has chosen to abandon forever.

Point of View, Style, and Tone in the Novel

One of Donleavy's characteristics as a writer is, as we have seen, his lyrical style. Since he uses the interior monologue to such a large extent, it is not surprising that the lyricism should quite often reflect the protagonist's feelings and emotions at any given time. One of the most lyrical passages in *A Singular Man* occurs at the end of the novel, when Smith is on the ship that is taking Sally's body away from the city for burial at sea. His interior monologue includes not only his impressions of the scene itself but also his very romantic reverie of the sea as an attractive resting-place for his beloved. The passage ends with his "prayer" for her, typical of the little verses or poems with which Donleavy frequently ends a chapter:

From the port stern side of this ship. See the horizon of thin white fingers with a sunlight glint of red and gold. Those were the tip top towers in which you [this is addressed to Sally] lived. Slip out from under that flag to the fishes dolphins whales, room to yawn and stretch. Command to fire the rifles. One splash in a rolling sea. And bubbles and wreaths are left. But maybe you'd like to know that at night seals sing. They come up out of the water with their big sad eyes.

> Good news
> In the sweet
> By and by. (pp. 303-304)

There are more lyrical passages, more sheer poetry, in *The Ginger Man* than in *A Singular Man*, partly because in the latter novel the unfriendly urban environment offers fewer picturesque scenes and inspiring moments to sing about. Nevertheless, Donleavy's bardic impulse makes itself felt in nearly every page of the work.

Another reason why the lyricism is muted in *A Singular Man* relates to the character of Smith himself. In keeping with his fear and uneasiness, the prose of his interior monologues is often given a "nervous," jerky quality that creates in the reader a feeling akin to Smith's own anxiety. Donleavy achieves this effect principally by using sentence fragments almost exclusively throughout the novel (except for the dialogue). Although sentence fragments are also an important stylistic feature of *The Ginger Man*, they appear much more frequently here and tend to be shorter and more abrupt. Note, for example, the brief paragraph that follows Smith's knocking the man onto the subway tracks in front of the approaching train:

> Crowd on the edge of the station platform. Train squealing and screeching. Yards ticking off. Hold my breath one year for each. Staring through the backs of all the heads. Silence. Voice shouting get back, get back. An elbow nudging Smith. (p. 184)

Smith is confused and alarmed, and the language of the passage conveys precisely the agitated rhythms of his mental processes.

An interesting aspect of Donleavy's manipulation of point of view—a strategy that he occasionally uses in his other novels as well—is his rendering of unpunctuated dialogue, interior monologue, and scenic description as stream of consciousness. Normally the dialogue in *A Singular Man* is conventionally punctuated (except for Donleavy's frequent practice of omitting question marks) and indented from the left-hand margin. But in one long passage the talk between Smith and Sally is written as if it were a part of the flow of Smith's thought. (There are times, as in the last passage quoted above, when voices other than Smith's are rendered as a part of his interior monologue, but they are clearly an element in the flow of impressions recorded as his stream of consciousness. In this instance, however, both Smith's and Sally's remarks to each other take the same form.) The occasion is the night they spend together after coming from Jiffy's party. When they begin their love-making, the point of view shifts from the dramatized scene showing them preparing for bed to Smith's interior monologue:

> Tomson smiling. Months of dreaming of this sun-flower. Opened now. Head rolling, a little ship back and forth on the sea, delicate white nose a sail. Long hands sliding down Smith's back. (p. 174)

A little later we are given Smith's brief observation on his good fortune with both his secretaries, followed next by unpunctuated dialogue:

> Two women in one day. Both my secretaries. Ports in storm. Smithy I'm breaking in two. Hold me together. Don't let me go. Or leave me. Even when it's coffin time. Smithy, not so loud, you poor poor guy. Let it go. Under the waves. Got your wrapped. Tickling me under the heart. It is. You rascal. Tell me a story. Were you ever honest. Sally. You see. Bonniface said at the University, realism was our friend. (p. 175)

At this point Smith begins the story of their escapade at college in the storeroom full of ale, but the point of view does not change. Until they are finished with their love-making, not only his interior monologue but also the story he tells and the comments from Sally are all woven together in the stream-of-consciousness manner.

Although the point of view makes us sympathize with Smith and see his problems as real human problems, Donleavy does not often attempt to describe Smith's world or the characters in it according to the conventions of realistic fiction. Instead of realism, with its accurately rendered surface details and its concentration on commonly observed life, Donleavy gives us his own personal vision of existence. Thus the novel has a certain fantasy-like quality, and Smith's life at times seems almost to be taking place in a dream. It is the dream-like (and sometimes nightmarish) atmosphere, which engenders insecurity and a feeling of helplessness in Smith, that especially makes this novel resemble the works of Franz Kafka. In particular, Smith's sense of being victimized and his perception of a puzzling and menacing world call to mind the plight of the protagonist of *The Trial*, Joseph K, who is innocent of any crime but nevertheless executed. The world of *The Saddest Summer of Samuel S* is also frightening and confusing to S, who—like Dangerfield and Smith—suffers from anxiety and a magnified sense of displacement. The influence of Kafka is clearly evident in the ominous and disorienting conditions of modern life that the protagonists of *The Ginger Man, A Singular Man,* and *The Saddest Summer of Samuel S* desperately try to cope with.[6] But that influence is more apparent in the latter two works because the dread experienced by the protagonists and the somber tone of much of Donleavy's writing are less relieved by humor than they are in *The Ginger Man.* Moreover, Smith and Samuel S lack the demonic energy and impulsiveness that keep Dangerfield from being overwhelmed; nor do they know the anarchic freedom that he often enjoys.

A Singular Man is in parts an extremely funny work. It has the farcical episodes, the bawdy humor, and the comic dialogue that characterize Donleavy's first novel. But the growing mood of melancholy that eventually overshadows the humor in his novels manifests itself strongly in *A Singular Man.* The note of sadness in the first novel is subordinated to its bawdiness, its explosively funny comic scenes, its many passages of brisk, humorous dialogue, and its roguish and unyielding protagonist. In *A Singular Man* there is much less comic dialogue. And the protagonist, for all his cleverness and financial success, is less defiant and rebellious, more given to dejection and pensiveness, and more withdrawn and resigned. The dark tone of *The Saddest Summer of Samuel S,* in which S's troubles drive him to despair and the brink of insanity, is but a deepening of the gloom that preoccupies Donleavy from the beginning of his career.

III. *The Saddest Summer of Samuel S*

The Saddest Summer of Samuel S (1966) is Donleavy's only novella to date. Because of its concentration on the pathos of the chief character, it resembles those sketches in the collection of short fiction called *Meet My Maker the Mad Molecule* (1964) that focus on the loneliness or dejection of a single figure. The predicament of Samuel S is even more trying than Dangerfield's, for Samuel is not only miserably poor but also middle-aged and without prospects for a brighter future. He is an American living in Vienna, and his major source of income is an occasional gift from rich friends in Amsterdam who send him money when he makes an appeal to them. He has been seeing a psychiatrist, called simply Herr Doctor, for five years in the hope of being cured of his neuroses. Although Herr Doctor tells him near the end that he is cured, S thinks that if he is ever normal there will be no way of actually telling. Thus his psychoanalytic sessions (he came to Europe to have them) prove to be inconclusive and disappointing.

Vienna itself does not please him either. Clerks routinely cheat him, suspicious eyes peer at him from doorways and windows as he walks down the streets, and people are in general unfriendly. He has an occasional companion, the Countess, with whom he has spent time pleasantly, but he alienates her by refusing the income she offers him. He strongly suspects that the conditions she will demand in exchange for giving him financial security will rob him of his integrity, and he haughtily rejects her offer without learning exactly what they are. It is at this point in his life that he meets Abigail, an American college girl traveling in Europe with her friend Catherine. She is fascinated with the

45

eccentric, aloof S and one day—after having toured Vienna with him—shows up at his apartment and offers to go to bed with him. Though he is lonely and would very much like to comply, he will not make love to her. He realizes that for her the episode would be only a kind of exotic adventure and resents the thought of being used for such a purpose. For himself, casual fornication would be dangerous, he thinks, despite the fact that Abigail is quite attractive. Samuel wants to marry and have children: he wants stability and a future, not another temporary relationship. Abigail, however, is too full of plans to consider marriage. She actually does entice him to bed, but without the promise of marriage he refuses to satisfy her. After a time S falls asleep, and Abigail revenges herself by biting him on the thigh and causing him to bleed. The next day she leaves, a day or two later S has his final session with Herr Doctor, and the novella ends with him in an agony of loneliness. As he leaves the Doctor's office in the last scene, he thinks of a dream he has had: he sees Catherine and Abigail off on a train, somehow falls under the wheels and is crushed as Herr Doctor and the Countess look on, and tries to die without screaming in pain and disgracing himself.

This dream—this final vision—is quite affecting and sums up much of the book's meaning. When Abigail leaves him, he has nothing to look forward to but old age and death. It is natural, therefore, that he would dream of dying as her train departs. He is a very vulnerable man, and he is by nature far from courageous, but throughout the novella he tries to endure whatever misery he cannot avoid without completely losing his dignity. (He does, of course, resemble Smith and Dangerfield in wanting to keep up a proper appearance no matter how desperate circumstances have become.) Thus in the dream his last moment of consciousness is the wish that he might die bravely and thereby gain the admiration of his friends. S is a defeated, despairing human being who is at last reduced to dreaming of nothing more than keeping a shred of dignity at the moment of death. Donleavy doubtless sees the desire to save face, to avoid shame and disgrace, as an ineradicable requirement of human nature.

S's Emotional Needs

The tale of S is sad in many ways. His "saddest summer" is but the culmination of an extremely depressing life. Donleavy does his best to wring our hearts by mentioning S's unhappy childhood and his sense of failure as an adult. When he was very young, no one gave him the affection and emotional support that he craved; as an adult, therefore, he lacks confidence in himself because he has no sure sense of personal worth. (Distressing childhoods also condition the adult lives of the protagonists in *The Beastly Beatitudes of Balthazar B, The Onion Eaters,* and *A Fairy Tale of New York.*) His value as a human being has not been reflected in the behavior of others. In addition, he is suspicious of any overtures of love from others because his experience has taught him that people are more likely to seek him out for their own selfish purposes than give him the unconditional love that he needs. Since he has lived his life feeling rejected, he naturally looks at human society from the perspective of an outsider. It is no wonder that he has developed eccentric habits and odd tastes. He has not, as an adult, been able to compensate for the insecurity and lack of love that marked his childhood. He has no job, no trade or profession, no firm plans for the future, and no intimate friend to whom he can tell his troubles. (He has an expensive psychiatrist instead.) Nothing promising lies before S, and he lacks the vigor of youth with which to begin his life all over. His every waking moment is a reminder that he is a failure. S's sadness is a form of despair.

In certain important ways *The Saddest Summer of Samuel S* reminds us of both *A Singular Man* and *The Beastly Beatitudes of Balthazar B.* In all three works the protagonist loses the girl in whose love he sees his last opportunity for a happy future. True, Abigail is not interested in marrying S, yet she represents his only hope for a love that would bring him contentment in old age. Sally dies and leaves Smith's life empty, and Balthazar suffers the loss of Fitzdare. But though Balthazar is as bereaved as Smith, neither he nor Smith faces the sort of crushing poverty that S endures. It is interesting that these three characters (like Sebastian) all share the very romantic notion that a woman's love offers solace, assuagement of life's griefs and sorrows. This notion implies that the love between a man and a woman is more than the mutual emotional fulfillment of two mature adults. It suggests that a man's happiness comes not by way of mutual sharing and sacrifice so much as through the reassurance and consolation given by a woman. It partakes more than a little of the child's attitude toward its mother and is very pronounced in Donleavy's works. Dangerfield, Smith, Balthazar, and S all at times feel (and act) like lonely, fearful little boys. (Much of *The Beastly Beatitudes of Balthazar B* concerns the protagonist's childhood, of course; but his loneliness, inordinate shyness, and total lack of self-confidence —which have their beginnings in his mother's indifference to him— persist into manhood.) It is significant that Smith makes love to Queen Evangiline, who is old enough to be his mother, and that Balthazar's first love affair occurs when he is twelve and Bella is a grown woman about twice his age.[1] And it is important to recall that S's emotional problems stem from a lovelorn childhood that to a great degree conditions his relationship with Abigail. Soon after she arrives at his apartment, S considers turning to her for the protection and comfort a child seeks with its mother:

> Sometimes one had to give oneself a big bear hug of sympathy. When no one else will ever wrap arms around you like a mother. And hold you tight and safe from harm. So close now. Do I throw myself panting on her chest and locked in sweat say marry me, wash my socks, grind my coffee bean, tint my toast the lightest warmest shade of brown. (pp. 62-63)[2]

A similar need is also felt by Sebastian, Smith, and Balthazar, all of whom want the sort of unqualified sympathy and tenderness that is normally associated with a mother's love.

The Earthy Female

Another ingredient that *The Saddest Summer of Samuel S* has in common with *The Beastly Beatitudes of Balthazar B* and *A Singular Man* involves the earthy, sexually aggressive, lusty female. (She actually makes her first appearance in *The Ginger Man* as Mary, the girl who surprises even Sebastian with her incessant demands for sex.[3]) This character, who is not the least bit shy about wanting to go to bed with the protagonist, possesses an attractive vitality because she honestly expresses her desires and offers the protagonist the physical pleasure he longs for. Mary, Sally Tomson, Abigail, Breda in *The Beastly Beatitudes of Balthazar B*, as well as both Rose and Charlene in *The Onion Eaters*, all differ from the conventionally "nice" girl in their utter frankness concerning sex. They are given to straightforward (and often risqué) talk when they make their desires known to the protagonist; and with the exception of Abigail and Rose, who are at least wholehearted in their wish to share the pleasures of the flesh, they are genuinely in love with him. Their enthusiasm for sex, moreover, and their open acknowledgment that they want to give themselves to him are never represented as depravity or immorality. In fact, Mary, Sally, Breda, and Charlene are quite natural and tender in their expressions of love. Abigail and Rose, while not exactly affectionate, are nevertheless sincerely passionate.[4] These girls are all far superior to the more limited, self-centered types that Donleavy gives his protagonists for wives—Marion, Shirl, or Millicent in *The Beastly Beatitudes of Balthazar B*. Samuel S has no wife to compare to Abigail, of course, but Abigail clearly fits the pattern of the earthy female. One of the points in her favor is that she has no ulterior motives in offering her body to S. The wives, on the other hand, want their husbands to conform to their ideas of proper behavior. They are harshly critical of their husbands, and they want to be supported by them. Abigail, Sally, Mary, and the other earthy females make few demands on the protagonist. For the most part, these girls simply want to be with him and enjoy sexual bliss with him. Abigail may be the least attractive of these characters because of her intention to stay with S for only a short time, but she is innocent of any mean-minded designs on him.

The robustness and honesty of the earthy females provide humor for the reader, and in *The Saddest Summer of Samuel S* most of the lighter moments occur when Abigail and S are together. Her unexpected biting of S's thigh (though cruel) is funny, just as the dialogue that they carry on is for the most part entertaining. But the novella has proportionately less humor in it than any of the full-length novels except *A Fairy Tale of New York*. Even in *The Beastly Beatitudes of Balthazar B*, in which the elegiac note is sounded throughout and finally leaves the most lasting impression, there are superlative comic scenes and a great deal of comic dialogue. And Beefy, Balthazar's Double, is one of the author's most witty and laugh-provoking characters. One reason why *The Saddest Summer of Samuel S* is so gloomy is that the length of the work does not permit the introduction of the large number of minor characters or farcical episodes that Donleavy includes in his full-length novels. Another reason, of course, is that the author concentrates on the unrelieved melancholy, or sadness, of his chief character. S is a man at the end of his rope, and even the humor of the bawdy scenes with Abigail is diluted by his anxiety. The humor is muted also in the scenes in which S and Herr Doctor appear together. S (though not so gifted with words as Sebastian or even George Smith) occasionally attempts witty remarks at the Doctor's expense, such as the following:

> "What's up Doc. Why you standing. Usually you're sitting at your desk. Someone spying on you from across the garden. Big purge of doctors who overcharge in Vienna, I hear." (p. 88)

S is not being flippant at all; the quip really reflects his discomfort and a desire to be friendly with his psychiatrist as much as it does a penchant for making jokes. Perhaps the funniest exchange between them occurs a few lines later, when the Doctor announces that he will no longer treat S:

> "Hold it, something's wrong Doc."
>
> "Yes Herr patient."
>
> "Maybe you heard I'm organising a union of patients for lower fees. Heh heh."
>
> "What I'm going to tell you Herr patient is something I do not want you to misunderstand. You are an extremely intelligent man and I do not think you will."
>
> "I am listening Herr Doc. What's your problem."
>
> "Herr S you are driving me nuts."
>
> "Whoa."
>
> "A sign that you are well and truly cured." (p. 89)

Again, S's uneasy feelings can be detected in his jesting, but the humorous reversal of roles between doctor and patient provides the dominant effect. At no point in the work, however, does the humor entirely free itself from the pathos of S's wretched situation.

The Saddest Summer of Samuel S might be called a mood-piece. Style, theme, and tone function almost perfectly as a unity to create a strong impression of S's forlornness and unhappiness—an impression that in turn evokes in us the feelings of pity and sympathy. Even the funny passages serve to make S more pitiable, because they reflect his ineptness and his very odd behavior. And the narrative style, with its heavy reliance on the interior monologue, brings us into direct contact with S's misery and sorrow. From a critical standpoint, therefore, the novella is a successful work. It departs from the two novels that precede it in its darker, more pessimistic portrayal of the struggle of the alienated individual trying to exist and maintain a psychological equilibrium on the fringes of society. And it points to the later novels in its depiction of a protagonist who is less resourceful and able to control the circumstances of his life than either Dangerfield or Smith and also less given to verbal playfulness and invention as a means of defense against the world.

IV. *The Beastly Beatitudes of Balthazar B* (1968),
The Onion Eaters (1971), and
A Fairy Tale of New York (1973)

These three novels should be discussed together for two main reasons: (1) Donleavy's style of composition remains unchanged in them. He still writes largely from the interior monologue point of view, though as in his earlier works of fiction he sometimes shifts—briefly and unobtrusively—to the limited, third-person point of view to give us a somewhat more objective picture of the protagonist. And he still relies very heavily on the sentence fragment as his chief technical device to approximate the mental processes of his protagonist. (2) These novels represent nothing fundamentally new in the way of theme or subject matter. Donleavy is once again preoccupied with the loneliness and sadness of his central character, with the unjust way he is treated, with the absurdity of the events he experiences, and with death as the overriding fact of existence. Much of what we find in these novels is actually a reworking of earlier ideas or an expansion of previously published material. In *The Beastly Beatitudes of Balthazar B* and *A Fairy Tale of New York* Donleavy continues to explore the melancholy state of mind that characterizes the protagonists of *A Singular Man* and *The Saddest Summer of Samuel S*. In addition, he portrays Cornelius Christian and Balthazar (like Smith and S) as victims of the cruelty and indifference of their fellows. (Like Smith, Balthazar and Cornelius also face the situation of having to carry on after the deaths of the women they love. In the case of Cornelius—to make matters worse—it is his wife who dies.)

A Fairy Tale of New York is an expansion of two earlier

works—the short story entitled "A Fairy Tale of New York," which is included in *Meet My Maker the Mad Molecule* (1964), and the play called *Fairy Tales of New York* (1961). Both *A Fairy Tale of New York* and *The Onion Eaters* are listed in *Contemporary Authors: A Bio-Bibliographical Guide to Current Authors* (1964), edited by James M. Ethridge, as works in progress. Thus they date from an earlier period in Donleavy's career than the publication of either *The Saddest Summer of Samuel S* or *The Beastly Beatitudes of Balthazar B* and suggest the necessity of his returning to older projects because he has—at least for the present—run out of ideas to begin another novel. This observation seems valid not only because *A Fairy Tale of New York* is an updating and reworking of two previously published works but also because both this novel and *The Onion Eaters* are distinctly inferior in quality to the long fictions that precede them in print. They lack the energy, the comic inventiveness, and—what is most important—the artistic control of these earlier works.

A Fairy Tale of New York starts off as the record of a grief-stricken young man who has just lost his wife; the tone is solemn, elegiac, and we feel sympathy for Cornelius. (The same tone is sustained in the short-story version and in the first act of the play, and in both pieces he claims our sympathy throughout.) Everything about him—his fine manners, his sensitivity, his suffering—draws us to him. But in the novel Donleavy inadvertently changes (or perhaps violates) the character of Cornelius. A considerable amount of the material that he adds in order to transform the short story and the play into a novel throws an unfavorable light on Cornelius and at times makes him positively unappealing. The unexplainably violent and sadistic side that we occasionally see in his personality, or the mean-spiritedness that is out of keeping with what we know of him at the beginning, completely erodes our sympathy. Thus *A Fairy Tale of New York* suffers from cross-purposes in the presentation of its protagonist.

The primary criticism to make of *The Onion Eaters* is that it has all the earmarks of an apprentice work. The progress of the action is difficult to follow—partly because individual scenes and episodes are incompletely developed and thus lack clarity, and partly because the sequence of events appears arbitrary and chaotic. The very large number of minor characters is confusing because many of these figures neither do nor say anything that helps us to differentiate them. Two major characters—Nails Macfugger and Rose—are rather carefully developed and play important roles in the first half of the novel, only to shrink to virtual insignificance in the second half. And, finally, the unity that might have been imposed by the point of view is missing because Donleavy cannot consistently sustain the illusion that we are witnessing the action through the consciousness of an observing protagonist (Clayton Clementine) whose particular sensibility receives impressions and colors the meaning of events in a distinctive way.

The Beastly Beatitudes of Balthazar B

Of the three novels being treated here *The Beastly Beatitudes of Balthazar B* is the most successful artistically. The chief characters, Balthazar and his friend, nicknamed Beefy, are delineated with consistency; the action develops clearly toward an appropriate conclusion; the tone and point of view are in perfect control; and at least two of the comic episodes—Balthazar's getting lost in Donnybrook (which results in his being arrested as an Arab) and Beefy's abortive attempt to smuggle girls into his college rooms to spend the night with him and Balthazar—are among the funniest Donleavy has written. Beefy himself, it is well to point out, is an extraordinarily funny and attractive fictional character. Not since *The Ginger Man* has Donleavy been able to offer a character with such witty command of language or a more delightfully mischievous manner.

The Beastly Beatitudes of Balthazar B is Donleavy's most lyrical and romantic work. At its center is the love story of Balthazar and the lovely Elizabeth Fitzdare, the girl he meets at Trinity College in Dublin and plans to marry. They spend many idyllic hours together at her father's large, wooded estate and find that they are perfectly suited to one another. They are rich, elegant young people who make each other very happy. Their marriage, which everyone eagerly looks forward to, promises to be an ideal one. But the wedding never takes place. Miss Fitzdare falls from her horse, sustains a grave injury, and before long dies.

Though at the time of the accident Balthazar knows only that their engagement has been mysteriously broken off by her representatives, the loss of his beloved completely shatters him. Unfortunately, it is only one of many occasions in his life when love is lost. His mother neglects him in childhood, his father dies when he is still quite young, and he is cared for by a nanny. He grows to love her as a mother, and she loves him too; but when he is sent from his home in Paris to a public school in England, he loses her as well. At school he meets Beefy, a puckish little boy his age whose given name is also Balthazar and who functions in the novel as Balthazar's Double. In almost all respects Beefy is Balthazar's opposite: a brilliant student, a bold companion who fears neither the cruel pranks of the other students nor the strict disciplinary practices of the masters of the school, and a randy wag even as a young boy who calls himself the "magnificent masturbator." He leads his quiet, timid friend into trouble, and both are sent down from school, each to go his own way. Again, Balthazar is parted from someone who is very close to him. But when he returns to Paris, he finds a new nanny, Bella, who falls in love with him. He returns her love, and they have an affair when he is twelve, though she is twenty-four. It is to Donleavy's credit that the affair is handled with such lyrical tenderness that it never seems salacious. They are right for each other emotionally, if not chronologically; she enjoys mothering him, and he is fully satisfied by her attention. He wants to marry her, but his mother—just returned from another pleasure trip—dismisses her. She and Balthazar never meet again, though a number of years later he learns that she has given birth to his son, whom he never sees.

When he enrolls at Trinity College, he not only becomes acquainted with Miss Fitzdare but also—to his great delight—finds Beefy again. The friendship with Beefy sustains him: Beefy, the Dionysian man who pursues every imaginable pleasure of the flesh, once more acts as a kind of mentor or guide to the Apollonian Balthazar, as is the case when they attend public school together. Balthazar's emotional losses—his psychic wounds—have left him unsure of himself, morbidly shy, and introspective. But Beefy, who is energetic and full of confidence, tries to bring him out of his shell by introducing him to the varieties of carnal gratification. Balthazar is too passive and timid to initiate a sexual liaison with a woman, but he does accompany Beefy to his rooms when Beefy decides that they must spend the night there with girls who will satisfy their every desire. (Beefy embodies the passion-driven, anarchic side of human nature that Balthazar lacks. Donleavy makes it a point to contrast Beefy's "diabolical" urges with Balthazar's "saintly" characteristics so that we receive the impression that together they represent a whole, balanced personality.) Beefy begins to disport himself with one of the girls, Rebecca, while Balthazar, who is with her companion Breda, looks on with astonishment. In the midst of his fun Beefy addresses the willing Rebecca:

> Pirouette my dear. Ah that raised some fine points. Of divinity if not law. But we're losing the sense of rape here. Cringe back a little my dear. If the Provost could only see us. Keeping up the fine traditions of the college. . . . And now. For rape.
> ....
> It's not fair of you to behave this way. Resist. For God's sake. O dear what can I do, my charm melts all hearts, and everyone, men women and children open their legs to me. Into the bedroom, Rebecca. I will lash you to the bed. (p. 192)[1]

But before Beefy completely indulges his "piggish proclivities" (as he at times calls them), the College authorities break down his door and put an end to the festivities.

The scene in the rooms is a masterful piece of comic writing and can be matched in this novel only by the hilarious episode in which Balthazar is accused by a woman in Donnybrook, a sex-obsessed harridan, of being an Arab who has come to her home in the night to rape her. This event, which causes Balthazar much embarrassment at Trinity when it is publicized in the papers, occurs after a date with Miss Fitzdare as he drunkenly tries to find his way in the dark from her uncle's house back to the College. These two comic interludes constitute the principal counterweights to the gloom that permeates the novel, though the presence of Beefy (and a few minor figures) in various other parts of the work provides occasional comic relief to the many long passages of interior monologue in which Balthazar's sad meditations are detailed. A rather tiresome feature of the novel is that too much space is devoted to Balthazar's almost uniformly melancholy thoughts, with the result that the important line of action that traces his growth from childhood to manhood and dramatizes the loss of love in his life sometimes slows to a halt. (The same weakness—the allotment of too much writing space to the protagonist's reflections in proportion to the action going on "outside" him— badly mars *A Fairy Tale of New York*, in which Donleavy must find something to say in order to inflate what originally was a play and a short story to the dimensions of a novel.) It is vitally important to record Balthazar's impressions and to leave us with a sense of his dejected state of mind, but this purpose could, it seems, have been achieved more efficiently.

Balthazar sees Breda home from Beefy's rooms and spends the night with her. She confesses her love for him, but he can do no more than feel an affectionate regard for her. It is sad that he cannot return her love because the earthy Breda is extremely kind to him and for a long time after their night together yearns for him. No woman will do for him, however, but Elizabeth Fitzdare. On the occasion of his visit to her father's estate, when they decide to marry, he enjoys one glorious night in bed with her and is as happy as we ever see him. He wants only to live with her in quiet dignity for the rest of his days. When he eventually loses her, therefore, he has nobody (except Beefy) to care for and withdraws more than ever into himself. (In fact, he actually loses his voice temporarily after the broken engagement because he feels utterly rejected and worthless. He does not learn of Miss Fitzdare's fall from the horse—and her subsequent death—until he has married Millicent.) After his plans with Miss Fitzdare have been ruined, his life is a steady psychological decline. He is tricked into marriage by the scheming Millicent and her parents, is viciously abused by her, and in effect is reduced to the status of a servant in his own home. Her only reason for marrying him, of course, is his money; and after she has spent a great deal of his fortune, she leaves him and takes their son. At the end even his selfish mother dies, and he is alone with no hopes for happiness.

Not surprisingly, Balthazar's Double, Beefy, also meets with unhappiness. For their little caper with Rebecca and Breda he and Balthazar are sent down from Trinity (thus repeating the pattern they establish at public school in England); and his wealthy grandmother, who has been supporting him, cuts off his allowance and disinherits him. In desperation Beefy decides that he must marry for money (a reversal of Balthazar's situation with Millicent) and courts Violet Infanta, whom he believes to be rich. He does manage to marry her—and enthusiastically leads her to try a few of his inventive sexual practices—but finds that she actually has no money. Still, he is more fortunate than Balthazar: he has Violet Infanta, whom he has meanwhile grown to love, and he still entertains some hope that he can convince his grandmother to change her mind about the money. Moreover, he still has his aristocratic aplomb and his clever tongue to help him get by in the world.

Balthazar has no financial worries, it is true, but neither does he have the desire to do anything further with his life. He barely possesses the will to live and imagines that the rest of his days will be passed in empty elegance. From earliest childhood he has been a poor little rich boy who loses those he loves, and now he sinks into melancholy—a defeated young man of kindly demeanor whose life is effectively at an end. Though there is much pathos in such a story, it is difficult to feel complete sympathy for Balthazar because he is so maddeningly passive and so abnormally shy. Donleavy makes him a gentle, retiring figure to whom things just happen, who is victimized time and again by the capricious workings of chance or the ill will and selfishness of other people. If he is meant to be a representative character, the author is apparently saying that even for someone rich and young nothing precious lasts. While this is no doubt objectively true, Balthazar's wealth and character set him apart from the mass of humanity, and it is thus easier to see him as a projection of Donleavy's own moroseness than as a figure who speaks for mankind in general.

A brief look at the three long fictions after *The Ginger Man* reveals Donleavy's intense absorption with the loneliness and depression of his protagonists and a growing tendency to strip them of the ability to handle their sorrow. Each of the protagonists who follow Sebastian Dangerfield—George Smith, Samuel S, and Balthazar B—carries a heavier burden of sadness than his predecessor; each is a little less aggressive and confident; each draws back from life a little more and seals himself off from contact with his fellows. And of course not one of them has the vitality or zest for life that Dangerfield displays. Dangerfield has many dark, anxious moments, but he also has the energy to defy adversity and a sense of irony that helps him to preserve his equilibrium. The amount of energy, the liveliness, that Donleavy assigns his next three protagonists after Sebastian decreases in each successive novel, just as the ironic detachment that he allows them progressively fades. In Balthazar these qualities disappear almost altogether, and Donleavy presents us with a static central character.[2] *A Singular Man, The Saddest Summer of Samuel S,* and especially *The Beastly Beatitudes of Balthazar B* thus show a steady decline in the creative dynamism and comic vigor of *The Ginger Man* and establish a pattern for the next two novels. (The protagonist of *The Onion Eaters* is as passive and withdrawn as Balthazar,[3] and both he and Christian in *A Fairy Tale of New York* are disappointingly dull figures without vitality or wit. The latter novel is severely weakened because little of Donleavy's comic gift—his strong suit as a writer—is evident.) Beefy of course fills part of the vacuum left by Balthazar's spiritlessness and is the finest achievement of *The Beastly Beatitudes of Balthazar B.* But the humor that he generates is eclipsed by the work's gloomy aspects. It is Donleavy's intention to stress Balthazar's woe, yet in carrying out his design he produces a fairly uninteresting protagonist.

The Onion Eaters

The plan for *The Onion Eaters* is a simple one. Clayton Claw Cleaver Clementine, a young American, inherits Charnel Castle from his great-aunt and moves to what appears to be a remote spot on the western coast of Ireland to inhabit it. As soon as he arrives there, a carload of very strange people descend on the secluded Castle and casually proceed to take up residence with him. Other visitors also show up from time to time who are just as mad or eccentric as the first ones, and by the end of the novel the unruly group has bankrupted him and burned down much of the Castle. The place itself and the basic framework for the action (the arrival of uninvited guests and the lunatic situations they precipitate) are vaguely symbolic: Charnel Castle (a kind of House of Death apparently representing the destination of all life's travelers) suggests a microcosm in which the insanities and obsessions of humankind destroy order, peace, and reason.

The absurd world of the novel is seen as a place of comic chaos. Clementine, like his famous ancestor who was known as Clementine of the Three Glands, has the curious distinction of possessing three testicles. His biological abnormality makes him unusual (and the object of intense interest to all who know of it); but at least he is sane and sensible, whereas most of the characters he encounters have something freakish or grotesque about them. Indeed, the visitors to Charnel Castle make it a veritable madhouse. Clementine hopes to lead a quiet life and to rest after a recent near-fatal illness; but he barely has time to be shown his rooms by his lively, lecherous old footman Percival before the mad scientists, Erconwald and his companions, knock at the door and subtly extract from him an invitation to be his guests. Though Clementine does not know it, his desire for a peaceful existence will never be realized, for the dotty experimentalists (as impractical in their pursuits as any of Swift's Laputans in Book III of *Gulliver's Travels*) bring disorder with them and in a short time virtually take over the Castle. Erconwald's colleagues are Franz Decibel Pickle, an expert in putrefaction, and George Putlog Roulette, a secretive physicist who is a descendant of the inventor of the scaffold. Erconwald himself seems to specialize in the gathering of any data related to sexuality (especially unnatural forms of sexuality) and, along with Franz, is interested in the manufacture of aphrodisiacs. All three of the men are vegetarians, and they give the novel its title because of the raw onions they eat. Accompanying them is a girl named Rose, upon whom they perform various of their experiments. Rose, who is coarse and anxious for physical rather than mental satisfactions, contrasts sharply with these researchers. She consumes great amounts of food and very quickly finds her way into Clementine's bed.

During the course of the novel the scientists set loose a number of poisonous snakes and dig for minerals in the Castle, ripping up some of the floors in the process. As if their presence were not disturbing enough, they are assisted in bringing about confusion by the friends who join them—Lead Kindly Light (named, of course, after the Protestant hymn), his wife, and three ex-convicts. Mrs. LKL (as Clementine thinks of her) and Rose immediately become deadly enemies and engage in mortal combat, with Rose at one point trying to strangle Mrs. LKL, who in turn attempts to shoot Rose with a pistol. Midway in the novel LKL, a surly and self-righteous madman, decides to blow up everyone who has gathered for dinner, releases a vial of nitroglycerin, and manages to destroy a large part of the dining hall and inflict injuries on a few of the characters. And late in the novel a terrible fire is started in the Castle when Erconwald gives LKL a hotfoot (in order to measure pain scientifically) and loses control of the experiment.

Clementine's nearest neighbors are Nails and Trudy Macfugger. Nails (as his surname suggests) is a randy character, a boisterous Anglo-Irishman who brings the novel much of its humor through his blustery talk. (Donleavy does a good job of parodying the speech of the Anglo-Irish gentry in his portrayal of this figure.) Clementine is a visitor at the Macfuggers' estate for a few days and accompanies Nails as he prepares to defend his property against a self-styled army of insurrection that is on maneuver in the area and has commandeered some of his lands. (The same army wishes to take over part of Charnel Castle.) The incredibly lascivious, middle-aged Victoria, who is immediately attracted to the much younger Clementine, is also a guest of the Macfuggers. (This woman keeps a photograph album of pictures she takes of penises and from the moment she sees Clementine wants to examine his genitals.) During the first night of their stay Victoria goes naked into Clementine's room on a pair of roller skates with a parasol in her hand. This ridiculous scene does not end with their making love; later, however, when Clementine goes to the city to do some business and enjoy a few days' respite from the lunacies of Charnel Castle, he has an affair with her. (He also poses for some of her pictures.)

After Clementine's stay with the Macfuggers the novel tends to lose coherence. A great many comic incidents occur, and a number of new characters are introduced; but no unifying pattern emerges from these incidents, and the minor characters are almost too numerous and indistinguishable from one another for us to keep track of them. (As stated above, Nails and Rose, both well-defined and important characters early in the novel, almost disappear after the half-way mark.) The funny scene in which LKL blows up the dining hall takes place just as Clementine returns to Charnel Castle; it is rapidly followed, however, by a much less successful sequence of comic events, most of which lack both the clear definition and the vitality of Donleavy's best scenes: a character named Bloodmourn fights Clementine's bull Toro with an umbrella and a coat, and the armor-clad LKL joins in with his lance; there is a testicle-squeezing contest between LKL and someone called Bligh in the dank tunnels beneath the Castle; Clementine and Trudy attempt to make love, but are interrupted when Bligh's boat filled with singing children is washed out to sea and must be rescued; Clementine and a makeshift crew set out in his yacht *Novena* to save them, but have to be towed back to shore; and three Americans—a couple called the Utahs and a girl named Gloria, who is constantly having orgasms—arrive at the Castle. It is at this point that Clementine decides to go away for a few days.

After a short interlude in the city with Veronica he learns from Bloodmourn that a part of the Castle has been destroyed by fire. When Clementine finds that he has no insurance to cover the loss, he and Bloodmourn, nearly penniless, begin to make their way back on foot. The journey takes several days, and the two are reduced to sleeping out and begging for food and rides. Clementine is now massively in debt and unable to repair the Castle, but he holds a large party for everyone in the neighborhood, including the soldiers from the army of liberation who have surrounded the place. The party itself is a madcap affair that ends in riot—an appropriate spectacle for the author's final reassembling of nearly all the twisted souls who have passed through the Castle during the novel. The day after the party Clementine is shown, in the last scene, walking by himself on an errand away from the Castle, puzzling over his experience in this strange land. He is without funds; he has no plans; and the servant-girl Charlene—the only girl who offers him honest love as well as sex—has disappeared. The ending is typical of Donleavy: the protagonist, who has been saddened and mystified by life, is all alone and unsure of what to do next. Only Dangerfield, of all Donleavy's protagonists, has the girl he loves at the end of the book and looks forward with any eagerness to the future. All the rest are lovelorn, dejected, and unhappy about what lies ahead.

A Fairy Tale of New York

It is instructive to examine the way that Donleavy uses the short story and the play on which this novel is based. *Fairy Tales of New York* dramatizes four episodes in the life of Cornelius Christian, whose English wife Helen dies on board ship as they are sailing to New York. In Act I Christian arrives in New York with the body of his wife and makes arrangements with the director of a funeral home, Mr. Vine, to bury her. The two become acquainted, and Mr. Vine, sensing an aptitude in Christian for mortuary work, offers him a job. Much of the time in this act is taken up with Christian's monologues in which he reviews his life with Helen and expresses his great sorrow that she is dead. Act II shows Christian being interviewed for a job in the offices of a manufacturing firm. Mr. How, the personnel director, is favorably impressed by him and arranges for Christian to talk with Mr. Mott, the owner. Christian's recent association with the Vine Funeral Home nearly causes Mr. Mott to turn him away, but in the end he is offered a position. In Act III Christian is working out with boxing gloves in a gymnasium. He is asked by the boxing instructor, Mike O'Rourke, to step into the ring with a character called the Admiral, a swaggering and bigoted older man, and pretend to be knocked out when the Admiral hits him. Christian reluctantly agrees, but is actually knocked unconscious by the surprisingly powerful Admiral. O'Rourke's joke backfires, and the hapless Christian lies sprawled on the mat at the end of the act. Act IV takes place in a restaurant, where the waiters refuse to serve Cornelius and Charlotte Graves, his date, because of the distasteful peach-colored shoes he is wearing. The smug waiters assume that the gaudy shoes could be worn only by an unrefined person—a person whose presence would detract from the exclusive atmosphere they are pretentiously trying to establish in the place. Charlotte is terribly embarrassed, she and Christian begin to quarrel, and he storms out the door, leaving her to face the cold-hearted waiters. Later he reappears, dressed in formal evening clothes and looking like a member of some exotic royal family—but with nothing on his feet except a couple of diamonds on his toes. He and Charlotte are then served by the now-fawning waiters, and Christian has his moment of triumph. In all four acts

Christian captures our sympathy because of his innocence, his suffering, and his vulnerability.

When Donleavy comes to write the novel, he uses these dramatic sketches as a basic framework for his story, but adds to them a number of new incidents and characters and develops in greater detail most of the characters he starts out with. Act I of the play ends with Christian and Vine leaving for the cemetery. In the novel, on the other hand, the episode is extended to include the actual burial of Helen. The opening three chapters that relate this material are almost word for word, with only a few insignificant changes, made up of the short story, "A Fairy Tale of New York." Also in the novel Donleavy shows Christian actually working for Vine, who becomes interesting as Christian's rough-spoken but compassionate friend, and learning the mortician's trade. It is through the tactic of having him work under Vine that Donleavy introduces the principal difference in the novel—Fanny Sourpuss. Fanny's third husband dies and is taken to the Vine Funeral Home for embalming. On the way to the cemetery Christian rides with her; thanks to Fanny's brazenness, they become well acquainted that day, and they sleep together that night. Thus begins an affair between the young mortician and the possessive older woman, who wants as much to be his mother as his lover. The affair continues throughout the novel, with Fanny—the crudest and most vile-talking of Donleavy's major female characters—pressing Christian to marry her and enjoy with her the great wealth her husband has left her.

In the novel Christian also has minor affairs with Mr. How's wife (who does not appear at all in either the play or the story) and with Miss Musk, Vine's assistant (who appears in both). The relationship with Miss Musk provides Donleavy with an occasional opportunity for writing Black Humor. She and Christian, for example, make love in one of the rooms where the corpses are treated. And Christian attempts a bit of grisly fun with her once when she is sitting near a corpse by placing one of its hands, which she thinks is Christian's, on her shoulder as a joke. (She faints from fright when she discovers the dead hand on her.) There is Black Humor too in many of the remarks Christian hears from Mr. Vine about the dignified nature of their business, in Christian's posing as a corpse in a casket for a publicity photograph, and in

Christian's handling of the first corpse he is allowed to prepare for burial. He is quite happy that Mr. Vine entrusts such an important duty to him, but he overdoes the make-up on the corpse's face and is sued by the dead man's widow for making her husband too good-looking.

The scene in court that eventually follows is quite funny—one of the few genuinely laugh-provoking passages in a book that is otherwise largely filled with morbidity, misanthropic bitterness, and sullenness. As mentioned in the introduction to this chapter, Christian's character undergoes a change in the material that Donleavy grafts onto the earlier works to make a novel. A great deal of space in the work—at least half—is devoted to Christian's interior monologues, in which he reveals his resentment at having been born into a poor family and orphaned at a young age and his angry conviction that people in general are despicable, dangerous, or unkind. He accepts as true what Mr. Vine says early in the novel—that homicide is nearly always the result of discourtesy. He feels smugly certain that a rude man he sees killed by an automobile deserves his fate. He is quickly moved to hatred and violence, and he viciously beats an employee in a bar who wants him to leave after causing a small disturbance. (In the novel he is a skillful boxer, despite what happens with the Admiral.) At other times he enjoys humiliating men who have bullied or insulted him. Donleavy tries to justify Christian's attitudes and behavior (which are often most unchristian) by placing him in a city that is filled with evil and inhumanity. In addition to the fatal automobile accident, Christian sees several people murdered, hears on the radio about many other killings, and constantly witnesses nastiness of every sort. The world that Donleavy projects is one of moral ugliness and spiritual ruin.

We are apparently supposed to believe that Christian is morally superior to the many contemptible people he sees, for he evaluates their conduct and pronounces heavy judgments on them; but he himself can usually be accused of lacking kindness and charity— and he never regrets the violence and suffering that he causes. In the four acts of the play and in the short story Christian is gentle, boyish, a little bemused; we have no trouble accepting him and feeling sorry that he has so many troubles. And we laugh with him when he cleverly manages a success or two. But in the pages that are added for the novel we gradually come to see him as an embittered, increasingly self-righteous (though of course victimized and unfortunate) character who grows to hate New York and most of the people in it and feels no guilt when he harms or disappoints others. On the contrary, he inflicts punishment with sadistic deliberateness—and obvious satisfaction—on those who mistreat him. When Fanny's second husband tries to chase Christian away from her early in the novel, for example, Christian twists the man's fingers, makes him kneel down, and then tells him to pray. Midway in the novel Christian is vilely insulted by a man on Fifth Avenue. Christian twists the man's arm behind him, forces him down on his knees, and declares that he is going to castrate him. Christian then adds that he will stab the man to death if he struggles. The threat is empty, and Christian walks away from him, but the revenge he takes on the wretch is itself odious. It is not possible to sustain the sympathy we have for him at the beginning of the novel, when his wife has just died, because his actions make him an unlikeable character. (Moreover, he very nearly forgets about Helen after the opening chapter.) We are reminded from time to time that the deprivations and miseries of his childhood explain his behavior as an adult, but the violence and quick temper given him in the material written for the novel do not fit with the mild-mannered ways that are carried over from the earlier pieces. Two contradictory impulses go into the making of his character, and he is thus the least credible of Donleavy's protagonists. He is also, by all odds, the least attractive. He is a belligerent, morose figure with whom we can finally have no fellow-feeling at all. The melancholy from which Donleavy's other central characters suffer in greater or lesser degree becomes in Christian a kind of unrelenting sullenness, a profound peevishness, that makes his work among the dead seem the only proper job for him.

At the end Christian, dispirited and thoroughly disenchanted with New York, sets sail for Europe. He has lost contact with Fanny, is all alone in the world, and faces an empty future. Donleavy's repetition of this same basic formula at the end of his long works of fiction after *The Ginger Man* does more than highlight his preoccupation with extreme loneliness and sadness. It also suggests a loss of faith in the possibility of finding viable human relationships or happy activities that can offset the inevitable defeats and disappointments in life. Dangerfield is surely at odds with the majority of mankind, and he has little to show for his twenty-seven years; but he has his ironic sense of humor and his special friends and, always, a woman to love. His future is uncertain, but it is not without promise. And it will not be experienced alone. In addition, he knows many satisfying ways of passing his time. He is full of vitality and lets himself be guided by a robust instinct for pleasure. But his near-heroic enthusiasm for life—kept intact, as we have seen, in spite of the terror of death—and his hearty enjoyment of companions are not shared by the subdued characters who follow him. They lack his talent for fully engaging life and his fierce determination to avoid death as long as possible. Something in Donleavy's other protagonists accepts the dominion of death without struggle. In the latest two novels Clayton Clementine and Cornelius Christian are virtual personifications of the death wish. Clayton barely escapes death when he is ill and recovers only to live in the House of Death. And Cornelius finds his true vocation in the work that death provides him. The subject of death becomes increasingly important in the Donleavy canon. It not only reflects the author's own compulsive brooding about mortality,[4] but also largely accounts for the steadily growing gloom in his fiction.

NOTES

I. *The Ginger Man*

[1] Robert Corrigan, "The Artist as Censor: J. P. Donleavy and *The Ginger Man*," *Midcontinent American Studies Journal*, 8 (Spring 1967), 60-72, gives a full account of the revisions Donleavy made in order to have the book published in America.

[2] John Stark, "Donleavy Beyond Culture," unpublished paper read at the Modern Literature section of the Midwest Modern Language Association meeting in Detroit, Michigan (November 1971), develops the idea that cultural pressures threaten the vitality of Sebastian and the protagonists of *The Saddest Summer of Samuel S* and *The Beastly Beatitudes of Balthazar B* as well.

[3] All page references are to *The Ginger Man* (New York: Dell Publishing Co., 1973).

[4] William David Sherman, "J. P. Donleavy: Anarchic Man as Dying Dionysian," *Twentieth Century Literature*, 13 (January 1968), 216-228, uses these terms to describe the character of not only Dangerfield but also the protagonists of *A Singular Man* and *The Saddest Summer of Samuel S*. Sherman, however, does not see Dangerfield and the others as alienated because "their lives are not socially relevant" (p. 216)—that is, they deliberately choose to isolate themselves from society.

[5] Arland Ussher, "Introduction," *The Ginger Man* (New York: McDowell, Obolensky, 1958), p. xi, says that the "sense of the Absurd" runs through the novel and sees Donleavy's humor as a response to it.

[6] Sherman, p. 216.

[7] Gerald Weales, "No Face and No Exit: The Fiction of James Purdy and J. P. Donleavy," in *Contemporary American Novelists,* ed. Harry T. Moore (Carbondale: Southern Illinois University Press, 1964), pp. 149-151, is the first scholar to point out the similarities among these three characters.

II. *A Singular Man*

[1]John Rees Moore, "Hard Times and the Noble Savage: J. P. Donleavy's *A Singular Man*," *The Hollins Critic*, 1 (February 1964), 2, says that Donleavy is ambiguous and leaves it up to the reader to decide whether George is an Everyman fighting for his soul or merely a "lunatic eccentric" whose view of the world is completely subjective. Sherman, pp. 221-222, sees George as the typical "man of the city" and the urban setting as "mythical."

[2]Dean Cohen, "The Evolution of Donleavy's Hero," *Critique*, 12, No. 3 (1971), 104, also states that Smith is paranoid.

[3]All page references are to *A Singular Man* (New York: Dell Publishing Co., 1973).

[4]Albert Camus, in "The Myth of Sisyphus," develops the idea of the absurd as the disparity between man's desire for order or meaning in his life and the universal disorder or chaos he preceives about him. See *The Myth of Sisyphus and Other Essays,* trans. Justin O'Brien (New York: Knopf, 1955).

[5]For a good discussion of the nature of the Double-figure in literature see Albert J. Guerard's introduction to and Claire Rosenfield's essay in *Stories of the Double,* ed. Albert J. Guerard (New York: J. B. Lippincott, 1967). Famous examples of the Double can be found in Conrad's "The Secret Sharer" and *Heart of Darkness,* Dostoyevsky's *The Double,* Stevenson's *Dr. Jekyll and Mr. Hyde,* and Poe's "William Wilson."

[6]That influence can also be seen in Donleavy's use of the single letter "S" for Samuel's last name and "B" for Balthazar's last name. In *Meet My Maker the Mad Molecule* he also has characters named Alphonse A, Franz F, and Gustav G.

III. *The Saddest Summer of Samuel S*

[1]Clayton Clementine, in *The Onion Eaters,* has a short affair with a woman who, as he recognizes, is old enough to be his mother—the randy Victoria. And in *A Fairy Tale of New York* Cornelius Christian has an affair with Fanny Sourpuss, who is not only old enough to be his mother, but also thinks of him as the baby she has always wanted but never had.

[2]All page references are to *The Saddest Summer of Samuel S* (New York: Dell Publishing Co., 1967).

[3]Arland Ussher's "Introduction" to *The Ginger Man*, pp. xv-xvi, identifies Mary as "Rabelaisian" and "earthy" and sees Sebastian as "the eternal essential Male."

[4]Christine in *The Ginger Man* resembles the earthy female in her enthusiasm for sex and in her real love for Sebastian, but she is not really aggressive and has an element of refinement in her character that sets her apart from the others. Fanny Sourpuss in *A Fairy Tale of New York* has the aggressive, lusty quality of the earthy female; but she is a generation older than any of these girls, is mean-minded and violent, and distresses Cornelius Christian by her possessive attitude and her demands that they marry.

IV. *The Beastly Beatitudes of Balthazar B,*
The Onion Eaters, and *A Fairy Tale of New York*

[1] *The Beastly Beatitudes of Balthazar B* (New York: Dell Publishing Co., 1969).

[2] Donald E. Morse, " 'Singed by an Impudent Fire': *The Beastly Beatitudes of Balthazar B* by J. P. Donleavy," unpublished paper read at the Modern Literature section of the Midwest Modern Language Association meeting in Detroit, Michigan (November 1971), also mentions Balthazar's passiveness and lack of ironic detachment as weaknesses in the novel.

[3] Thomas LeClair, "*The Onion Eaters* and the Rhetoric of Donleavy's Comedy," *Twentieth Century Literature,* 18 (July 1972), 168, comments on the "static" quality of Clementine and claims that his excessive passivity and vulnerability (which are inadequately accounted for) are serious flaws in the novel. See also p. 173.

[4] Thomas LeClair, "A Case of Death: The Fiction of J. P. Donleavy," *Contemporary Literature,* 12 (Summer 1971), 329-344, not only traces the theme of death in Donleavy's long fictions through *The Beastly Beatitudes of Balthazar B,* showing the enormous effect on the protagonist that his awareness of death has, but also calls the author's predisposition to treat this theme a "virtual obsession" (p. 329).

BIBLIOGRAPHY

The Works of J. P. Donleavy

The most recent paperback editions of Donleavy's works (which have been used in the preparation of this study) are listed below, along with the place of publication, the date, and the publisher of the original editions of the same titles.

NOVELS

The Ginger Man. New York: Dell Publishing Co., 1973. Originally published in Paris in 1955 by Olympia Press.

A Singular Man. New York: Dell Publishing Co., 1973. Originally published in Boston in 1963 by Atlantic-Little, Brown & Co.

The Beastly Beatitudes of Balthazar B. New York: Dell Publishing Co., 1969. Originally published in New York in 1968 by Delacorte Press.

The Onion Eaters. New York: Dell Publishing Co., 1972. Originally published in New York in 1971 by Delacorte Press.

A Fairy Tale of New York. New York: Delacorte Press, 1973.

NOVELLA

The Saddest Summer of Samuel S. New York: Dell Publishing Co., 1967. Originally published in New York in 1966 by Delacorte Press.

SHORT FICTION

Meet My Maker the Mad Molecule. New York: Dell Publishing Co., 1968. Originally published in Boston in 1964 by Atlantic-Little, Brown & Co.

PLAYS

> *The Plays of J. P. Donleavy.* New York: Dell Publishing Co., 1972.
> Also published in New York in 1972 by Delacorte Press. Includes
> *The Ginger Man* (first produced in 1959), *Fairy Tales of New
> York* (first produced in 1960), *A Singular Man* (first produced in
> 1964), and *The Saddest Summer of Samuel S* (not yet produced).

ESSAYS

> "Traveler, Consider My Dublin. . . ." By J. P. Donleavy as told to
> Richard Joseph. *Esquire,* April 1967, pp. 122, 208.
> "What They Did in Dublin." Introduction to *The Ginger Man: A Play
> by J. P. Donleavy.* New York: Random House, 1961, pp. 3-41.
> Reprinted in *The Plays of J. P. Donleavy.* New York: Dell
> Publishing Co., 1972, pp. 6-37.

Secondary Sources

Camus, Albert. *The Myth of Sisyphus and Other Essays.* Trans. Justin
O'Brien. New York: Knopf, 1955.

Cohen, Dean. "The Evolution of Donleavy's Hero." *Critique,* 12, No. 3
(1971), 95-109.

Corrigan, Robert A. "The Artist as Censor: J. P. Donleavy and *The Ginger
Man.*" *Midcontinent American Studies Journal,* 8 (Spring 1967), 60-72.

Guerard, Albert J., ed. *Stories of the Double.* New York: J. B. Lippincott,
1967.

LeClair, Thomas. "A Case of Death: The Fiction of J. P. Donleavy."
Contemporary Literature, 12 (Summer 1971), 329-344.

_____. "*The Onion Eaters* and the Rhetoric of Donleavy's Comedy."
Twentieth Century Literature, 18 (July 1972), 167-174.

Moore, John Rees. "Hard Times and the Noble Savage: J. P. Donleavy's *A
Singular Man.*" *The Hollins Critic,* 1 (February 1964), 1-11.

*Morse, Donald E. "Singed by an Impudent Fire: *The Beastly Beatitudes
of Balthazar B* by J. P. Donleavy." Unpublished paper read at the
Modern Literature section of the Midwest Modern Language Association
meeting in Detroit, Michigan (November 1971).

Sherman, William David. "J. P. Donleavy: Anarchic Man as Dying Dionysian."
Twentieth Century Literature, 13 (January 1968), 216-228.

*Stark, John. "Donleavy Beyond Culture." Unpublished paper read at the
Modern Literature section of the Midwest Modern Language Association
meeting in Detroit, Michigan (November 1971).

Ussher, Arland. "Introduction." *The Ginger Man.* New York: McDowell, Obolensky, 1958, pp. ix-xvi.

Weales, Gerald. "No Face and No Exit: The Fiction of James Purdy and J. P. Donleavy." *Contemporary American Novelists.* Ed. Harry T. Moore. Carbondale: Southern Illinois University Press, 1964, pp. 143-154.

---

*Copies of these papers are available at the Midwest Modern Language Association, English/Philosophy Building, The University of Iowa, Iowa City, Iowa 52240.

Date Due
